The Practice of Structured Analysis

Exploding Myths

Robert Keller

The Practice of Structured Analysis

Exploding Myths

Robert Keller

Yourdon Press
1133 Avenue of the Americas
New York, New York 10036

Library of Congress Cataloging in Publication Data

Keller, Robert, 1939-
   The practice of structured analysis.

   Includes bibliographical references and index.
   1. System design. I. Title
QA76.9.S88K44   1983   001.64   83-62140
ISBN 0-917072-31-6

Printed in the United States of America

Library of Congress Catalog Number 83-62140

ISBN: 0-917072-31-6

This book was set in Times Roman by YOURDON Press, 1133 Avenue of the Americas, New York, N.Y., using a PDP-11/70 running under the UNIX® operating system.*

---

*UNIX is a registered trademark of Bell Laboratories.

Dedication

The Practice of Structured Analysis: Exploding Myths is dedicated to all those managers, end users, and analysts who must make the structured approach work in the real world.

Acknowledgments

Many have helped me give birth to this book. Particular thanks are due to Nancy for typing the illegible first drafts and to the exceptional editorial staff of Yourdon Press: Wendy, Janice, Susan, and Jacob.

Thanks for her patience and encouragement are most warmly given to Clare.

Contents

The Practice of Structured Analysis

Exploding Myths

Robert Keller

Introduction

From the time the computer emerged as a business tool until recently, business people who wished to automate were forced to mold their business needs to fit the limitations of computer hardware and software. Now, with nanosecond cycle times, multimegabyte memories, and programs that speak natural, conversational English,* the computer has become a truly useful tool, approachable by the least technically trained people. Users today have the right to expect what they ask for. In short, computerized applications now can be driven more by users' needs than by technological limitations. However, along with this increased user friendliness comes the responsibility for business people to know how to ask for what they want, and for analysts to know how to write down what the users ask.

With the invention of structured analysis, which specifies business functions independently of computers, users gained an ideal medium to specify their information needs. In addition, technical people gained a tool with which, finally, they could specify systems precisely, completely, and without redundancy.

Approaching a structured project

Skillful execution of a structured project requires an understanding both of the underlying theory of structured analysis and of its application in practice. The definitive texts on structured analysis generally give the theoretical ground rules for conducting a structured project. What they don't do completely is to guide project personnel through

---

*INTELLECT is a natural English database query facility developed and marketed by Artificial Intelligence Corp., Waltham, Mass. As far as I know, it is the only commercial natural English system and is well worth investigating.

the myriad of unpredictable circumstances that don't quite fit the theory.

A theory is an ideal, a framework, like a formal system in mathematics; it can be realized in practice in many different ways, although it is not itself a real thing. Scientists evolve theories based usually on some experimental evidence, but engineers are required to make theories work in the real world. The structured analyst is such an engineer, applying the theory of structured systems development to some particular real-world situation.

Many of the questions I hear as a consultant relate to whether an analyst *has* to do something that the published literature defines to be part of a structured analysis. The answer is unequivocally no. After digging into the theory and understanding the basic principles of structured analysis, the analyst chooses those ideas that can benefit one system and discards those that don't make sense in a particular situation.

Here are a few examples of the principles of structured analysis and some circumstances that may cause you to modify them in practice.

- A primary output of a structured analysis is a well-defined set of logical data files; the theory propounds an elaborate method for deriving these files from existing physical files. BUT you do not have to do a full-blown logical file derivation if the eventual file structure is given or is self-evident.

- Every lowest-level process on a data flow diagram needs an unambiguous description that will allow writing an executable procedure for it; the theory encourages the use of structured English for this purpose. BUT you do not have to write structured English when some other unambiguous process description is more acceptable to the user.

- The theory strongly urges postponing until the very end of analysis the specification of physical characteristics such as record layouts. BUT you do not have to leave physical constraints out of your logical system description if they are givens.

Data flow diagrams, data dictionaries, and structured English are some of the tools of the structured revolution. But they are only tools; the process of analysis, the completion of a structured analysis, is more than using the tools. The process includes not only interviewing the users and understanding the spirit of the system that is to be, but also skillfully negotiating the interplay between the users' wishes and the constraints imposed by a real-world operating environment. Structured analysis theory can't advise you here, and that's one reason you can't rely on it completely. Therefore, you should not feel constrained to follow the theory exactly, but rather you must bring all of your past experience to bear on solving the problem at hand. No theory is so complete that it does not require modification and amplification. Use the tools where they fit; discard the ones that don't fit.

About the book

The Practice of Structured Analysis: Exploding Myths is, in a way, a summary of the dos and don'ts of structured analysis. It provides the practical guidance for approaching a structured project and for developing close cooperation between management, analysts, and end users. The book reviews the early life of a structured project, from organizing the user community to stepping into a structured design, and contains practical suggestions for the smooth implementation of a structured analysis. At each step, I have noted things that can go wrong, things that don't *have* to be done according to the structured methods, and things my experience says you must do if the project is to succeed. It is the distillate of several thousand hours of consultation and teaching, of working with users, managers, and analysts struggling to make practical use of a new methodology in their own work.

The Practice of Structured Analysis: Exploding Myths can be read easily by any person who has studied the basic concepts of structured analysis, and it provides enough of an orientation to basic concepts so that it can be read by those who have not been exposed to the structured approach. Although the book often seems to address the analyst primarily, it is intended for an audience composed of analysts, users, and managers. In the text, my view is that of a consultant, addressing myself at different times to the different types of reader. This changing viewpoint underscores the essentially cooperative nature of a structured analysis. All of the players must work as a team to complete a successful structured project.

I approach the subject of structured analysis in three ways: by presenting an overview in Chapter 1; by reviewing the basic tools of structured analysis in Chapters 2, 3, and 4; and by looking at the process of structured analysis in Chapters 5, 6, 7, and 8.

In Chapter 1, I look at some of the general aspects of systems development: why projects get into trouble, whose fault it is or isn't, and how using the structured approach helps to avoid problems.

Chapters 2, 3, and 4 present the basic tools of structured analysis: data flow diagrams, project dictionary, and techniques (such as structured English) for describing the changes presented pictorially by the data flow diagrams. The discussion presents the basic principles in fairly elementary form so that a person who is unfamiliar with them can appreciate issues surrounding their application. The main focus, however, is on the issues that arise in trying to apply these tools, and on helping the practitioner to use them effectively and with minimal effort.

In Chapter 5, I present some aspects of the structured project life cycle that don't get much emphasis in textbooks because step-by-step procedures have not been developed for them. In particular, I discuss the integration of the system into an existing business, and who does what in a database design and when they do it. Giving explicit attention to these items in the structured life cycle ensures that they aren't ignored as the project proceeds. The chapter also includes an overview of the steps in a textbook structured analysis; this serves as a preface to the following chapters, which examine the steps in detail.

Chapter 6 addresses some human issues that are peripheral to the actual technical development of a structured specification. These issues include the organization and management of a structured project, including the use of the team concept, and the training of end users and managers. Chapter 7 looks once again, in depth this time, at structured analysis as a process. In reviewing each step in the process, both for the current and the new system, I examine the actual technical development of the structured specification.

In Chapter 8, I discuss techniques for deriving a set of logical files and give suggestions for simplifying the logicalization process. In a brief conclusion, I offer some final thoughts on structured analysis and its benefits to contemporary systems development personnel.

1

Structured Methodology:
Its Context and Goals

People have been developing computer systems for more than thirty years. Nevertheless, up until the last decade or so, no determined effort had been applied to treating systems development as a discipline in its own right. Now, with the coming of the structured techniques, systems development has indeed evolved into an organized discipline.

This chapter begins with some general statements about the nature of systems development. It further explores why traditional development methods have failed to provide adequate solutions to systems needs and why a structured approach can help to overcome these failings.

1.1 Systems development as a hero journey

Throughout the ages, the heros and heroines of myth and fairy tale have embarked on journeys in search of some goal or treasure that is often apparently impossible to attain. I like to look at systems development as a kind of hero journey, because drawing an analogy between the systems development process and a journey in classical mythology helps me to set goals and shows me that the trials and tribulations that plague each project are a natural part of the human experience.* The analogy suggests also that if you have clear goals the project is likely to have a happy outcome, usually better than expected if the hero pursues the objectives faithfully.

The cycle of change shown in Figure 1.1 depicts the fundamental stages experienced by a participant in any situation of change and growth, whether the participant is a hero on a fairy tale journey or a member of a systems development project. In this cycle, a person begins in a state of satisfaction with the status quo, often bordering on complacency. As the situation changes, he moves sequentially through periods of chaos, insight, and integration. Finally, a new stable state emerges, and eventually a new cycle of change begins.

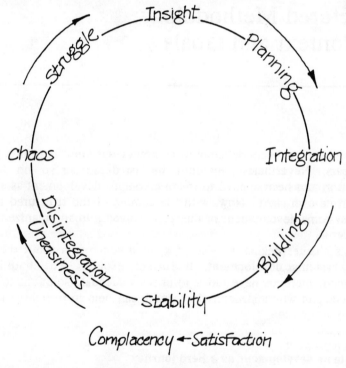

Figure 1.1. The cycle of change.

---

*The hero journey has been described eloquently by several writers. In particular, J. Campbell's *Hero with a Thousand Faces,* Bollingen Series XVII (Princeton, N.J.: Princeton University Press, 1972), and E. Rossi's *Dreams and the Growth of Personality* (New York: Pergamon Press, 1972) have clearly related the work of the classical hero to the problems of modern times.

1.1.1 Stability: the setting for change

In daily life, we rely heavily upon the predictability of certain situations. That is, we make assumptions that some things will not change, and this allows us to put our energies into those other things that do require our attention. This approach to living is necessary, and if we are attentive to those circumstances that will change, responding to change can be relatively painless.

Yet, we often become complacent and fail to notice that some of our assumptions are no longer valid. This is as true for the information environment we work in as it is for anything else. You may have noticed that we often become so comfortable with the way things are that we prefer not to notice that the garage roof is leaking, or that the numbers in the monthly summary report we rely on are no longer meaningful. When complacency sets in, it's almost as though we intentionally ignore imminent problems in the hope that they'll go away.

1.1.2 Chaos: the price of inattention

It is at just this point of complacency that something happens, often accidentally, to radically change the situation: The garage ceiling caves in, or inventories run out at a warehouse that was supposedly fully stocked. There follows a period of chaos when the old complacency is shattered, and no clear direction for the future remains.

In a systems environment, this is the time when a feasibility study is conducted and analysis begins. To return to our analogy, during this phase the hero (sometimes an analyst, sometimes an involved user) must pursue the ultimate goal of bringing clarity to the often murky state of the user's business. The systems building project is a journey that you make from where you are to where you want to be. Clearly, if you don't know where you're starting or where you're going, you'll probably get lost. The purpose of analysis is to define your starting point and destination.

During the journey, the fairy tale hero often must slay dragons, which represent those situations in daily life that preserve chaos. In a structured project, these dragons often appear at the beginning of a project in the form of the analyst's or user's determined resistance to documenting the existing system. Then, project teams find that when the time comes to specify the new system, inadequate documentation of the current system becomes a stumbling block to further progress. Another danger might be the user's refusal to admit that the current system is inadequate.

1.1.3 Insight: halfway home

The important characteristic of the successful hero, who finally achieves the goal of restoring stability, is the ability to persist in dealing with these and other dragons in the struggle to discover the final solution. During systems development, this often means tirelessly revising data flow diagrams (DFDs), updating the project dictionary, and writing and rewriting descriptions of processes during the analysis stage.

By persevering in developing accurate DFDs, and in carefully maintaining a project dictionary, you will finally be able to present a complete, unambiguous, nonredundant, and heroic specification of what needs to be done to regain a stable situation. The completed specification of the system to be designed and constructed represents the midpoint of your journey.

1.1.4 Integration: the last battle

The remainder of the hero's journey is bringing home the prize so dearly won. The second half of the journey in a systems development project consists of the work of structured design and implementation; the prize is the successfully operating new system.

On the road home, the hero encounters such difficulties as inadequate resources to build all that has been specified, or the temptation to change the system without maintaining the specification. To produce and implement a good structured design, this part of the journey requires just as much watchfulness as did the earlier road of trials. Nevertheless, as long as the hero remains alert and has a clear systems specification in hand from structured analysis, success is virtually assured.

1.2 Why unstructured projects fail

Finishing systems late, producing systems that don't do what the user expects, and going way over budget are a few of the typical failings of traditional systems development efforts; most people who embark on a structured project are intimately familiar with these inadequacies. I have summarized some of the most common complaints about traditional systems development techniques below, focusing on the kinds of things analysts, users, and managers have to say about each other. In many cases, the complaints point out the ways in which projects tend to fail. These complaints are taken from real life, and I have heard them all more than once.

For example, the analyst and project manager complain that the user doesn't know what the current system does, doesn't know what's needed for the future, keeps changing the goals of the project, and isn't interested in what the systems developers are doing; the user and analyst complain that the project manager tries to freeze the specification in a fluid environment and cares about politics only; and the user complains that the analyst wants him to sign off on incomprehensible documents, doesn't understand his business, and can't show him a model of his new system.

These complaints reveal several reasons for a project to fail or at least get into trouble. First, it is not unusual for project goals to change during the course of developing a system. In fact, given that every business situation is dynamic by nature, change is guaranteed. The problem with traditional development methods is that specifications are generally incomplete, ambiguous, and redundant, and, therefore, difficult to change.

Second, most traditional development methods provide no way of enforcing the specification of clear, objective goals for the project. This causes problems when the business environment changes. In such a case, the goals of the project should be rewritten to fit the new environment. If the goals are fuzzy to begin with, it will be difficult to determine how they should be changed.

A third problem arises from the lack of a medium for organizing information gathered at user interviews. As a consequence, reviewers fail to cover such disorganized material completely and accurately.

Unfortunately, project members beset by these problems typically won't stop to improve communications or define goals and the attitude of pushing-through-no-matter-what comes to the fore. It would be better for management to cancel the project, and save what time and money it could.

One further complication arises when role responsibilities become fuzzy. If the user tries to tell the project manager how to run the analysis team, or if the manager tries to prevent further changes to the specification in order to meet a schedule, or if the analyst tries to tell the user how the business runs, then these people are interfering where they don't belong.

1.3 Why structured projects succeed

People have been writing computer programs for more than thirty years, but not until the last decade or so has any determined effort been applied to treating the development of computer programs as a discipline in its own right. One of the major contributions to making this a formal discipline has been structured systems development.

What is structured systems development? It is a discipline that produces a concise, unambiguous, nonredundant, and thorough specification of a system using, among other tools, graphic data flow diagrams. The DFD-based specification is supported by brief, narrative, though structured, English descriptions of processes, by logical database descriptions, and by a complete data dictionary for the project. This structured specification of the user's needs is converted to modular structure charts during design, which in turn are transformed into structured programs during implementation.

Since its inception in the early 1970s, structured systems development has become widely accepted. Sparked by pioneering publications from Warnier, Constantine and Yourdon, Jackson, Gane and Sarson, and DeMarco, thousands of analysts, designers, and programmers are applying the structured techniques in their own work.*

1.3.1 What is structured analysis?

Structured analysis plays an important role in the success of structured systems development. The goals of structured analysis listed below follow naturally from a need to solve the problems of unstructured systems described above. Not only are these goals "official" goals of structured analysis, but they must be satisfied by any successful project. Structured analysis is intended to provide a common communication medium between user and analyst, a means to model the user's system early in the project, and a maintainable specification, which is nonredundant, unambiguous, and complete. The result is that structured analysis enhances the chances of easily automating the system the way the user wants it.

1.3.2 Role responsibilities

Structured analysis solves the problem of role responsibility in projects by clearly defining the duties of the user, analyst, and project manager in systems development. A brief summary of who should do what in any project follows.

The manager's job is two-fold: first, to mediate the interchange of information between user and analyst; and second, to provide an environment conducive to complete exploration of the user's needs.

---

*J.D. Warnier, *Logical Construction of Programs,* 3rd ed., trans. B.M. Flanagan (New York: Van Nostrand Reinhold, 1976); E. Yourdon and L. Constantine, *Structured Design: Fundamentals of a Discipline of Computer Program and Systems Design,* 2nd ed. (New York: Yourdon Press, 1978); M. Jackson, *Principles of Program Design* (New York: Academic Press, 1975); C. Gane and T. Sarson, *Structured Systems Analysis: Tools & Techniques* (New York: Improved System Technologies, 1977); T. DeMarco, *Structured Analysis and System Specification* (New York: Yourdon Press, 1979).

The user and the analyst do the actual specification work. The analyst's primary duties are to write down a precise definition of the user's business by taking a complete inventory of data and the changes that happen to data. After that, the analyst helps the user to define clear goals for the project and to document both the current and new systems.

The user's main responsibilities are to know and to communicate the details of the business being analyzed and to take an active interest in changing the current system to a system better suited to the business. This means the user must be available to the analyst, be open to the possibility of change, and be willing to define clear, objective goals for the project.

1.3.3 Benefits of structured analysis

The encouragement of user participation is a major benefit of structured analysis; it helps prevent error and confusion. I remember a meeting of a group of systems people regarding a project that was in chaos because no one understood the user's needs. The manager opened the meeting by saying, "Having lost sight of our objectives, we must redouble our efforts!"

This obviously counterproductive approach is evident in project after unstructured project. Systems staffs insist upon compounding ignorance of the user's business by misunderstanding the information they do have. In contrast, practitioners of structured analysis produce accurate specifications of the user's needs because structured analysis forces communication between users and analysts.

The structured approach to analysis has numerous other benefits for analysts, users, and managers, but most attractive are those features that help the users and systems developers to

- conquer a complex problem by dividing it into simpler, smaller problems that can be solved independently

- plan and model a system before it is built

- use a minimum number of tools for specifying the system

- finish on time, as specified, and within budget

- have a highly maintainable system at implementation and installation

We can now see why systems developers need structured analysis and how its characteristics make it a widely used technique.* Among its other benefits are that it produces models of the system early in the development stages and it produces a specification that is primarily graphic, and therefore easily comprehended by both analysts and users. Although structured analysis is usually described as a rigorous methodology, the structured approach allows us the freedom to iterate over (that is, repeat) a phase or a series of phases as often as necessary.

In the next chapter, I look at the raw material of structured analysis, data. I clarify what data are and how they behave, and show how data items are defined in structured analysis.

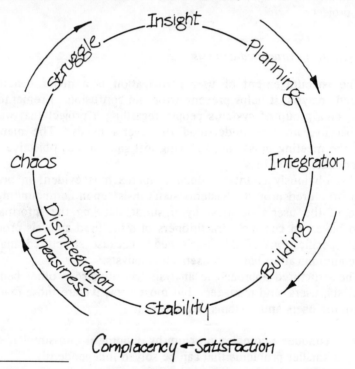

*I strongly recommend that you engage an *experienced* structured consultant to work closely with your team on its first structured project. There are several firms and a growing number of independent consultants who now have extensive experience with structured systems. Alternatively, or in addition, you may wish to contact one of the user groups such as the Structured Methodologies User Group, which I started in Philadelphia. These groups are composed of representatives of companies engaged in structured projects; because they work with issues that may be of concern to you as well, they can be a source of practical wisdom. Numerous live and programmed courses on the principles of structured analysis, design, and programming are also available. Some of the companies offering such training are Deltak (Chicago), Brandon Systems (Bethesda, Md.), Yourdon (New York City), McAuto-IST (St. Louis, Mo.), and Datapro Research Corp. (Delran, N.J.). In addition, extension programs in structured analysis are beginning to appear at universities and colleges across the country.

2

Data: Definition,
Notation, and Storage

To do any work in systems development, users and analysts need to understand what the word *data* means, how data are defined in a system, and how data differ from processes. This chapter addresses these issues as they apply to a structured analysis, and forms the basis for the discussion of data flow diagrams and process specification in the following two chapters.

2.1 Data defined

One characteristic of data is that data are things of some kind, things to which changes happen. When talking about an item of data, one senses that it is something static. Moreover, physical data are static things that can be picked up, looked at, and used. Informational data, such as the title of the book, tend to be somewhat intangible. As Table 2.1 shows, data, whether physical or informational, can generally be named by a noun, such as *book* or *amount*.

Following Table 2.1 are some examples of data in each of their three most common states: resting, moving, and being transformed. Chapter 4 looks in more detail at the processing of data and the types of data change most commonly observed in systems.

Table 2.1
Examples of Physical and Informational Data

Physical data	Informational data
book	title, author
egg carton	manufacturer, brand name
paycheck	date, amount
Report 21B	Current Month Sales

Data resting
- The eggs (data) are in the refrigerator (file for data).
- The Sales Report (data) is in my file.

Data moving
- I'm getting the eggs from the refrigerator.
- I'm sending the Sales Report to the sales manager.

Data being transformed
- The egg is becoming an omelet (transformed data).
- The Sales Report is becoming a Monthly Summary (transformed data).

2.2 Data and processes compared

Although data are static entities, they can move from one location to another or be transformed into other data. When data are moved or transformed, some *process* is acting on the data, since data do not change by themselves. A process usually can be described by a verb (the action) and a direct object (the data being acted upon).

It is difficult, perhaps surprisingly so, for people to clearly understand the difference between data and processes. This difficulty is not restricted to nontechnical people. I have seen numerous systems people write down a process named Bills without the faintest recognition that a bill and the paying of a bill are distinct: The first is data; the second, the processing of data. The important difference to keep in mind is this: Data are things to which changes happen; a process makes changes happen to data.

2.3 Physical and logical defined

In order to understand what data and processes are, we must understand the structured analysis use of the words *physical* and *logical,* which are used to describe data and processes. In the terminology of structured analysis, the meaning of *physical* and *logical* may differ somewhat from the common understanding of these words. The difference between physical and logical is the same as the difference between the way things are and the way you would like them to be ideally.*

Physical generally means *implementation dependent.* A physical file is a file of data described as it appears on a physical medium such as a disk, a tape, or a piece of paper stored in a file cabinet. The physical nature of a file limits the form and use of the data it contains: The data take the form of a certain number of characters in a particular format and are available only through specific physical access methods, such as reading a disk or opening a file drawer.

By contrast, *logical* means *implementation independent* and is used to describe data or a process from which all implementation-dependent characteristics have been removed.

A physical process may be a computer program or a specific set of manual steps carried out by a person in the real world. A DFD that contains mostly implementation-dependent physical data and processes, and that shows mainly physical inputs and outputs is referred to as a *physical DFD.* A DFD that shows mostly implementation-independent data and processes is called a *logical DFD.*

In a structured analysis, there is an evolution from a primarily physical description of an existing system to an informational description of the new system and finally to a predominantly physical description of the new system. Even in the final structured specification, however, it is unusual for a DFD to be completely physical or completely logical. To try to remove all implementation-dependent characteristics from intermediate DFDs is both frustrating and unnecessary.

---

*The term *logical* is inaccurate since most logical entities on a DFD imply nothing concerning the subject of logic. This issue arose in a class attended by a high-level manager who was also a skilled logician. The more I used the term *logical* in our structured analysis sense, the more he would protest: "It's not at all logical." He explained to me the logician's understanding of the word *logical* and insisted that I not use it to mean something else. We finally settled on two alternative words: *informational* for logical data and *functional* for logical processes. I now use these terms interchangeably, including the word *logical* because of its common usage in the jargon of structured analysis, but the meaning is to be construed as functional or informational.

2.4 Physical data

Since the computer is an information processing device, physical data are usually represented in the computer by their informational content. But it's important to realize that physical items can be data in their own right as well as contain information about the item itself. A book, for example, is an item of data in a system that requires placing books on shelves. In addition, the book contains information such as title, author, and so on. In some systems, the DFDs must depict both the physical item (the book), as well as show its informational content (the title).

To give an example of a system whose specification carries physical data, I will describe the business of a client I once worked with. The client's business was to build automated warehouses. In such a system, the conveyor belts are, in actuality, physical dataflow paths connecting processing nodes where a package may be wrapped, labeled, and so on. The informational content of the physical items (the name and address, for example) are carried with the package. Care must be exercised to treat the package and its informational content separately, since they are likely to be processed separately in many ways. Nonetheless, since handling the physical data is part of the system, the physical data must be shown even on the logical DFDs.

2.5 Defining data

In addition to understanding what is meant by *data,* we must be able to define any item of data, physical or informational, in such a way that another person or a computer program can recognize and process it. To do this in a structured project, we maintain a dictionary of all data that appear anywhere in the system.

2.5.1 A notation for defining data

In order to promote uniformity and to eliminate ambiguity and redundancy, a rigorous notation has been developed for defining data. The notation uses the symbols shown below, and is exemplified in the definition of Paycheck that follows. These constructs are both necessary and sufficient for describing any item of data; in principle, no others are required.

Notation for defining data		Repetition variations	
=	Consists of	Any number	$\{\text{Friend}\}$
&, +	AND	One or more	$_1\{\text{Friend}\}$
$\begin{bmatrix} \text{item} \\ \text{item} \end{bmatrix}$	OR	Up to 3	$^3\{\text{Friend}\}$
{}	Repetition	From 1 to 3	$^3_1\{\text{Friend}\}$
( )	Optional		
* *	Comment		

Dictionary definition of Paycheck and its elements

```
Paycheck   =   *Gift from payroll dept. on payday*
           =   Stub + (Check)

Stub       =   *Record of pay and deductions*
           =   Date + Amount + ₁{YTD Total} + ₁{Deduction}

Deduction  =   ⎡ Withholding-Tax ⎤
               ⎢ FICA            ⎥
               ⎢ United-Fund     ⎥
               ⎢       ⋮         ⎥
               ⎣                 ⎦

Check      =   *Negotiable pay*
           =   Date + Payee + Amount
```

Note the inclusion of the comment in the definition of Paycheck. Such a comment, while certainly not rigorous, contributes to a general understanding of the data, which is sometimes clouded by the rigorous definition that follows the comment. Paycheck consists of Stub and, optionally, Check.

The Stub constituent of Paycheck is further defined to include certain items, one of which (Deduction) is defined even further. A deduction consists of either Withholding-Tax or FICA or others. The other, optional constituent of Paycheck (Check) is also defined in terms of its constituents.

For entries such as Paycheck, some of whose constituents are defined further, we use the term *data structure*. An entry such as Deduction is referred to as a *data element* because it is defined in terms of the values it can take in the real world; such values are not defined further in the dictionary because their meaning is considered to be self-evident. In effect, data structures are shorthand notations for combinations of data elements. Every entry in the dictionary eventually must be reducible to data element definitions if we are ever to get a system to work. Here is an example of the difference between a data structure and a data element.

Data structure   Transaction-Id = Product-Id + District-Code

Data element   District-Code = $\begin{bmatrix} 01 \\ 03 \\ 07 \\ 14 \end{bmatrix}$

Notice that in the definition of Paycheck there is a natural transition from physical data (Paycheck, Stub, and Check) to the informational content of these items (Date, Payee, and Amount). This evolution from physical to informational is typical of structured analysis and is, in fact, one of its goals: to transform physical data and processes into their informational and functional equivalents, respectively, for processing by the computer.

Because the data dictionary notation is both necessary and sufficient for describing data, it illustrates one of the benefits of structured analysis: It uses the minimum number of tools in producing a structured specification. Using this notation has the significant advantage of minimizing the complexity of the method, thus making it easy to learn.

A disadvantage of using the simplest possible notation is that descriptions can become cumbersome. One way in which many projects have sought to extend the dictionary notation is by introducing an inclusive OR construct. The definition of Funds at the left uses the necessary and sufficient notation, and at the right is an equivalent definition with an inclusive OR (|) symbol.

Necessary and sufficient	*Inclusive OR*
Funds = $\begin{bmatrix} \text{cash} \\ \text{check} \\ \text{cash + check} \end{bmatrix}$	Funds = [cash | check]
Means to use any one	Means to use one or any combination

Clearly, the second, extended method is more compact. This simple extension saves considerable space and often improves readability of the dictionary entries. Project members can certainly make other extensions, but only after carefully evaluating the consequences. It is counterproductive, for example, to add a simplifying notation that is ambiguous.

2.5.2 Definition detail

Now that we know how to define items in terms of their constituents as done in structured analysis, an important question arises as to how detailed such definitions should be. Clearly, one could define any item either in very general terms or down to the level of its molecular structure. The answer is that the level of detail needed to describe each item depends on what we wish to do with it. Since different parts of an item of data may be processed in different ways, each part may need to be described at a different level of detail.

An egg is a good example. If we are describing the cooking of an omelet, we assume that most people know what an egg looks like: "Egg" is an adequate description. On the other hand, if we wish to make a meringue, we must know that the egg has both a yolk and white since these constituents are processed separately.

The following list shows several data and at least one way of describing each in terms of its constituents. The list contains a further breakdown of the yolk of an egg; this level of detailed understanding is needed, for example, if we wish to do a biochemical analysis of the egg.

Egg	= Yolk + White
Book	= Cover + Pages
Paycheck	= Check + Stub
Report 21B	= District + Sales-Code + Current-Month-Sales
Yolk	= Protein + Carbohydrates + . . .

The depth of detail in the data description depends heavily on the user's view of the data, for it is the user who determines the elementary items of data during analysis.

Be careful, however, not to simply accept the user's choice of depth for defining data, since most users and managers are not attuned to data processing issues in data description. The analyst understands the processing of data and must often coach the user to the level of detailed data description appropriate to a particular system. For example, if the analyst asks a user, "What is customer?" the user may respond, "What d'ya mean, what is customer? A customer is a customer; anybody knows that!" Or, he could respond that a customer is many different things: the person sold to, the location shipped to, or a parent company. He may even use the data dictionary format, writing his response as

Customer = Last-Name + First-Initials + Address

The first response is more typical than one might think. "Customer" is such an intrinsic part of a user's understanding of the business environment that to give it a definition seems unnecessary to him. When coached for a second definition, a user can easily describe different types of customers and their characteristics. For structured analysis, it may be important to persevere until the user offers the third description, which contains components that may eventually become items of data in a computer system.

2.5.3 An exercise

If you have never tried using the dictionary notation, you may wish to do the following exercise. First, list several different physical data items that you process in your business or personal life. Second, choose one item and describe its components completely using the notation presented in this book. Try to be as precise as possible. For example, if you choose to describe your paycheck, note that what you get from payroll is not a paycheck, but a window envelope plus a paycheck.

It doesn't matter what items you choose to describe, since the dictionary notation is completely general. It does matter, however, that you choose data and not processes. When you describe the data's contents, be careful to ensure that the components listed for an item are in fact part of the item, and to limit the amount of detail in your descriptions.

2.6 The project dictionary

Data definitions are stored in a document often called the *data dictionary*. The name can be misleading, since there frequently is also a company-wide data dictionary, used to store information about all of the company's data; this dictionary is managed by a database administrator and is often maintained by a database management system. To describe the working dictionary used on a specific project and to differentiate it from a company-wide data dictionary, I prefer the term *project dictionary* for what DeMarco calls a data dictionary.* Eventually,

---

*T. DeMarco, *Structured Analysis and System Specification* (New York: Yourdon Press, 1979), p. 125.

much of the project dictionary may be merged into the larger data dictionary, but it is kept separate during most of the structured development project.

2.6.1 The dictionary's content

Theoretically, all documentation goes into the project dictionary, although noting physical constraints, such as data formats and storage media, in the dictionary is generally unnecessary during most of a structured analysis. This is true because analysts try to ignore physical constraints when building some of the important products of structured analysis. For example, one such product is a functional description of a system that fits the needs of the business, but is independent of a particular implementation. Including physical details too early unnecessarily binds the project to a limited technology.

The lists below are not exhaustive, but they do give a flavor of the many different types of information that can be included in the project dictionary.

Project dictionary entries	Definitions may include
— Data elements — Data structures — Files — Processes	— Narrative comments — Formats — Volumes — Samples — Standard names

The examples presented below show the essential information to be kept for each major type of dictionary entry. In all cases, the item being defined should have a unique name that is used to refer to the item on data flow diagrams. If possible, choose names that give a clear idea of the meaning of the item even without your looking up the definition. For processes, the name should consist of an active verb followed by a single direct object.

In the examples, process numbers indicate where data, files, and processes can be found on data flow diagrams. It is usually best to wait until late in the analysis to include these numbers, since frequent DFD revisions can turn already difficult dictionary maintenance into a clerical nightmare. On the other hand, process numbers can be very useful for cross-referencing data flow diagrams to processes.

In all cases, some definition of the item is needed. The definition varies for each type of item and it need not always follow the structured methods rigorously. For example, if you wish to describe Sales Report #21, it may be a good idea to include a sample page from the report as well as use dictionary notation to describe its content. However, whatever definition you include must be complete and unambiguous; ideally, it should also be nonredundant.

As another example, in defining a Payee data element, which can be any of the company's 50,000 employees, including the employee list in the dictionary is pointless. It is far better in such a case to use the dictionary to point to the corporate employee list, which is maintained elsewhere.

Data element examples

Name:	District
Alias:	District Code
Values:	01 *Los Angeles*
	02 *New York*
	03 *Chicago*
	: :
	: :

Name:	Budget-Amount
Alias:	
Values:	0 to 50,000

Name:	Payee
Alias:	Employee
Values:	*See Corporate Employee List*

Data structure example

Name:	Check
Alias:	
Connections:	3.2 − 3.3
Composition:	Date + Payee + Amount

File example

Name:	Employee-History-File
Alias:	
Connections:	To 4.5, From 3.2
Access:	Random by Employee-Number
Composition:	{Employee-Number + Name + Address +
	. . . }

Process example

Name:	Update Employee-History-File
Number:	4.2
Description:	*structured English, structured flowchart, or decision table*

2.6.2 Dictionary maintenance methods

There are primarily three ways to store and maintain definitions in the project dictionary: manual, semiautomated, and fully automated. No matter what technique is used, the dictionary *must* be kept up-to-date if the project is to proceed smoothly.

2.6.2.1 Manual project dictionary

In very small projects, a completely manual method can be used successfully. This amounts to storing dictionary definitions in a looseleaf notebook and placing a single definition on one sheet of paper in the formats of the examples shown above. The entries can easily be kept in alphabetical order. It's also easy to include sample report formats, DFDs, and other pictorial material.

The major disadvantages of the manual method have to do with the sheer bulk of a dictionary with more than a few hundred entries, particularly when you want to look at the entries in other than alphabetical order. I have used this method successfully, but would recommend it only when the project life cycle time is short and when the number of entries is fewer than about three hundred.

2.6.2.2 Semiautomated project dictionary

With the present proliferation of word processor and spreadsheet programs, particularly on microcomputers, a much more desirable method is to store dictionary definitions in the computer. In this scheme, even a high-quality text editor program can suffice. The analyst must still alphabetize the entries and insert cross-references himself.

This method is good for larger projects, although it requires some modification of the dictionary notation discussed earlier. In particular, the system cannot represent large square brackets containing alternative data structures or elements. For this case, I use a list of the alternatives separated by a vertical bar (I) and enclosed in small square brackets ([]).

The main advantages of the semiautomated method are that it stores many entries in a fairly compact form and uses other computer programs to sort the entries for special listings. As with any automated method, a separate looseleaf binder probably will have to be used to keep any sample reports or other pictorial material.

Its restrictions notwithstanding, this is my favorite method for maintaining a project dictionary.

2.6.2.3 Fully automated project dictionary

Many companies use fully automated database management systems (DBMS) for controlling computerized production data on a company-wide basis. Generally, these packages include facilities for maintaining data definitions and for producing various listings of the dictionary contents. Some are even oriented toward storage of process descriptions and DFDs.

A DBMS is theoretically an ideal medium for storing the project dictionary. In the real world, however, I have often found these systems to be more trouble than they are worth. The reasons are twofold: First, company data dictionaries are intended to maintain long-term records of relatively stable production data. Database administrators are often reluctant to allow the dynamic structured project environment to encroach on their stable environment. Second, the time between submission of a change to the company data dictionary and its appearance in the dictionary is likely to be long, often a matter of days.

From my point of view, these two factors generally rule out the automated data dictionary as a viable medium for the structured project in progress. However, at the end of the project, project dictionary entries will probably have to be integrated with the company's data dictionary; therefore, analysts should be aware of the requirements of that dictionary so that they can mold project dictionary definitions to fit easily into the company's data dictionary.

The single most important caveat on a structured project is to keep the project dictionary up-to-date along with the data flow diagrams that show processing. Whether you use a manual or automated system for maintaining the dictionary, the system is all but worthless if the dictionary is not kept current with the diagrams it supports.

2.6.3 The project librarian

Any nontrivial structured project needs one person who is solely responsible for making changes to the project dictionary. This person is called the project librarian, and should possess an exquisite blend of technical and clerical competence. Among the project librarian's responsibilities are drawing and balancing DFDs, detecting aliases, and proofreading the project dictionary after it has been entered. As far as I know, few if any projects have found the ideal project librarian, that person who has some technical competence and can also tolerate the possibly boring details of maintaining the project dictionary. Some of the better ones are entry-level programmers, particularly those who have previously held clerical data processing jobs such as keyboarding.

2.7 Summary

In this chapter, we have studied the raw material of all computer work: data. We have defined the term, discussed a notation for describing data, and looked at various methods for storing descriptions of data. Finally, we have discussed that all-important aspect of a structured project, the project dictionary.

Now, with an understanding of data in their static state and of ways to describe them, we can look more closely at data flow diagrams, the graphic structured analysis tool for representing the dynamics of data.

3

Data Flow Diagrams

The data flow diagram is the primary tool of structured analysis for showing graphically the processing of data. Not only is it used for describing the user's business, but it is also the common language for discussions between users and analysts. Specifically, the DFD provides the user with a notation for recording changes in data, for documenting his business, and for telling the analyst what he wants. These reasons alone should convince users of the merit of learning to draw DFDs. An end user who can draw, or at least understand, data flow diagrams is an invaluable asset to a project. Such a person speaks a language that the analyst understands; he thus makes possible free communication about the business rather than hindering the process of analysis by misinterpreting models or needing long explanations of what the models say. Let us look now at DFDs in detail.

3.1 DFD components

Figure 3.1 illustrates the notation of DFDs. The square boxes marked S represent a *source* of or a *sink* for data. A source could be a clerk entering payroll data, a different computer system providing raw input to the system, or any other entity that feeds unprocessed data into the system being analyzed. A source provides a particular item of data (X in Figure 3.1), but the diagram does not indicate where the source got the data or what processing was done to it previously.

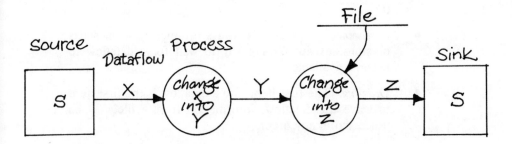

Figure 3.1. Schematic DFD.

A sink is any entity that consumes the data the system produces. Again, the diagram does not show what the sink will do with the data; we know only that a certain item, Z in this case, is sent to the sink.

Processes in a data flow diagram are represented by circles containing some text. The text describes in very general terms the one function performed by that process. The types of processes are discussed in detail in Section 3.3.

The line marked File represents a place where data are stored. In the physical world, this file could be in the form of magnetic tape, file cabinet, or even someone's shirt pocket; in any case, the file is a resting place for data when not being used by a process.

Processes, files, sources, and sinks are interconnected by lines with arrow heads called *dataflows*. They represent pipelines for passing data from one place to another. The dataflow is a kind of storage since more than one item of data can be in the pipeline simultaneously.

3.2 Rules for drawing DFDs

By giving them names, I have formalized most of the rules underlying the drawing of DFDs. Although I seldom refer to these rules by name during a project, this kind of categorization seems to help students learn the technique. There are six rules:

- *Conservation: Only* those dataflows can leave a process that can be made from the inputs into the process.

- *Parsimony:* A process should have *no more* inputs than it needs in order to generate the outputs.

- *Independence:* Each process knows only its own inputs and outputs, *not* where they are coming from or going to.

- *Persistence:* A process is always running; it never starts or stops, except temporarily to wait for a dataflow to become available.

- *Ordering:* The first item into a dataflow is the first item to leave the dataflow; information from a file may be processed in any order.

- *Permanence:* Using an item from a dataflow removes it from the dataflow; using information from a file does *not* remove it from the file.

People new to structured analysis have little appreciation of the implications of these rules, particularly of the third and fourth rules. In order to illustrate each rule's meaning, I present examples of the rules applied to practical situations.

3.2.1 Conservation rule

The principle of *conservation* requires that the only outputs from a process are those that can be generated using its inputs. In Figure 3.2, conservation of data means that if Funds and Deposit-Slip are put into a process, the process will produce only something that can be made from the inputs, say, Bank-Deposit. Funds alone or a Deposit-Slip alone would not be enough to prepare a legitimate Bank-Deposit.

In addition to illustrating conservation of data, Figure 3.2 introduces the idea that there is more than one kind of process: One kind merges dataflows into a new dataflow and one kind changes our view of the same dataflow. Valid is shown in parentheses to indicate that the validating process has not affected the contents of the dataflow. I enumerate some different kinds of processes in Section 3.3.

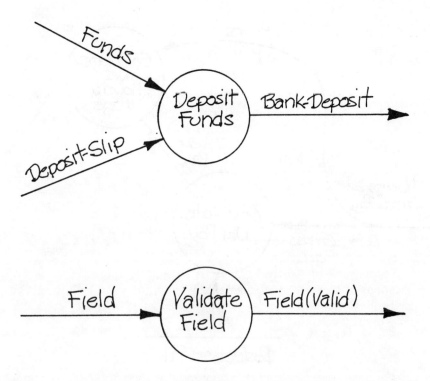

Figure 3.2. Example of conservation rule.

3.2.2 Parsimony rule

The principle of *parsimony* requires that a process have only those inputs that it uses to produce its outputs.

Figure 3.3 illustrates the idea that a part of a dataflow not needed by a process (Hours in this case) should bypass that process (Calculate Net Pay). This splitting of dataflows raises a practical problem of synchronization. That is, eventually the split-off data may have to be synchronized with other pieces of the original dataflow.

In practice, synchronization is crucial. Since a process such as Calculate Net Pay could discard an invalid instance of Gross-Pay, there needs to be some way of communicating that information to the Calculate Net Hourly Wage process. Too often, the detection of this problem is left to a walkthrough late in the project, in which it is bound to come up. It is far better to deal with it while preparing the DFD.

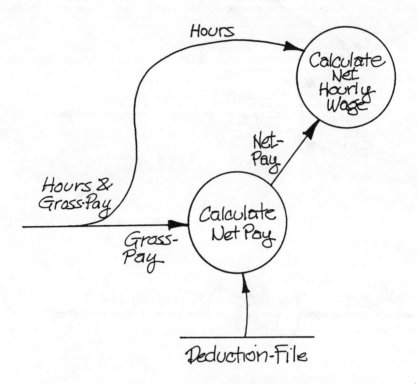

Figure 3.3. Example of parsimony rule.

I have seen this synchronization ensured in these ways:

- The analyst attaches to both Hours and Gross-Pay some common identifier that can be checked by Calculate Net Hourly Wage as Net-Pay arrives for processing. This is perhaps the cleanest approach since it violates none of the principles of DFDs.

- The analyst assures that Calculate Net Pay always puts out a Net-Pay for every input of Gross-Pay. If Gross-Pay is in error, then a null value of Net-Pay is the output. I don't much like this method, since it requires

an understanding between the two supposedly independent processes of the meaning of a null value. While
null can be defined in the project dictionary, it has no
particular meaning to the business under analysis.

- The third and least theoretically acceptable method is
to allow Hours to go through the Calculate Net Pay
process even though it has no purpose doing so. This
concession to practical convenience almost always
creates maintenance problems in the final system. I
strongly recommend against this method.

In any case, it is worthwhile noting in the project dictionary those
places where identifiers have been added, or null values used, or any
other contrivance employed for the purpose of synchronization.

3.2.3 Independence rule

The principle of *independence* requires that a process be oblivious
to all parts of the system except those determined from its own inputs
and outputs. This principle means that so long as its input and output
data definitions don't change, a process can change drastically in how it
accomplishes its function without affecting any other process.

Independence of processes is at the crux of producing highly
maintainable systems. The most serious maintenance problems in systems result from changes that affect processing in other parts of the
system, and the failure to recognize or document these effects on other
parts. By ensuring at the structured analysis stage that processes are independent and that data shared between processes are well documented, the analyst makes the system easier to change later on.

Figure 3.4 shows that the Validate Input Field process receives
dataflows from two different sources. Validate Input Field is independent because it not only doesn't know where its input comes from, but
really doesn't care. Its only concern is that there is a field waiting to be
validated according to certain known rules. Independence is perhaps the
most difficult of the DFD rules to put into practice.

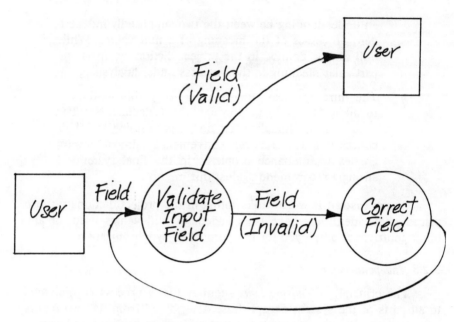

Figure 3.4. Example of independence rule.

3.2.4 *Persistence rule*

The principle of *persistence* suggests that a process is ready to run whenever an input dataflow appears. The Translate English into French process shown in Figure 3.5 can be purchased as software at your local microcomputer store. The translator program (when running) exemplifies persistence in that it is always ready to do its translation process and waits at the point at which an English-Word input is required.

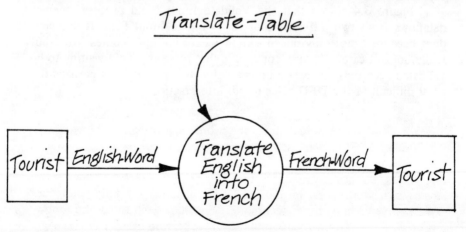

Figure 3.5. Example of persistence rule.

3.2.5 Ordering rule

The principle of *ordering* states the sequence in which data from a dataflow or file can be processed: The data in the dataflow are processed in the order in which they arrive, whereas the data in the file can be accessed in any order.

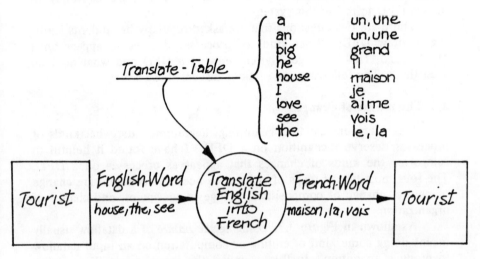

Figure 3.6. Example of ordering rule.

The example in Figure 3.6 illustrates that the first word in a dataflow is the first one processed and the first one to be output. Notice also that the entries in the file Translate-Table can be stored and accessed in any order.

3.2.6 Permanence rule

The principle of *permanence* describes the susceptibility to destruction of data in dataflows compared to data in files: The data in a dataflow disappears after being processed, whereas the data in a file can be read without being affected.

Once again the Translate English into French process is a good illustration. As shown in Figure 3.6, once the tourist has put a word into the English-Word dataflow, the word is processed and vanishes. By contrast, the Translate-Table entries remain unchanged no matter how often they are accessed.

These six principles are all that you need to know to draw DFDs. However, if you're new to drawing DFDs, practice will help you to become comfortable with the technique: You may wish to try the following exercise, but don't overcomplicate it. The whole point of the exercise is to give you a feel for drawing circles joined by lines and for naming them. (Remember that there is almost always more than one correct way to diagram a particular system and that it's up to the user and analyst to decide which way best describes the business.)

For this exercise, consider a system that updates transactions to a Master-File and produces an Audit-Trail. The exercise is simply to draw a DFD to reflect this system.

There are two questions that are asked regularly by students learning to draw DFDs: What kinds of processes deserve to appear on a DFD? and, How do I get started drawing a DFD and what do I do after that? The following two sections discuss these issues.

3.3 The nature of change

It is often unclear to a beginning diagrammer just what kinds of processes deserve recognition on a DFD. I have found it helpful to categorize the kinds of changes that appear as processes on a DFD. The four most typical types of change we need to document are change of nature, change of composition, change of viewpoint, and change of organization.

As shown in Figure 3.7, *changing the nature* of a dataflow usually means doing some kind of editing or computation on an input dataflow to produce an output. In this example, the input, originally in dollar values, is transformed to a percentage. The input apple has unequivocally become an output orange, so to speak.

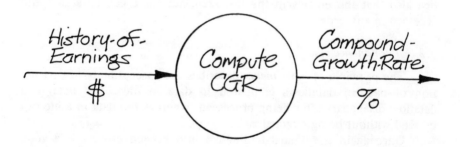

Figure 3.7. Change of nature example.

As in Figure 3.8, a process that causes a *change of composition* actually makes no change in the basic nature of the input data. This type of process simply takes one input and separates it into its constituents to produce two or more outputs. Conversely, a change of composition process could appear as two or more inputs, Check and Deposit-Ticket, that are joined in a straightforward way to produce a single output, Bank-Transaction.

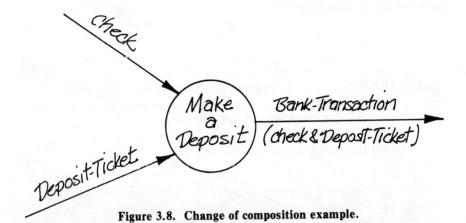

Figure 3.8. Change of composition example.

The *change of viewpoint* example in Figure 3.9 also involves no actual changes to the data. With this type of process, an input will probably also appear as an output. The only difference in this example is that Check-Register has been reconciled. In the diagram, Reconciled is placed in parentheses to indicate that the output dataflow is identical to the input. This means that there is no need to make an entry in the project dictionary for Check-Register (Reconciled), assuming that Check-Register has been defined.

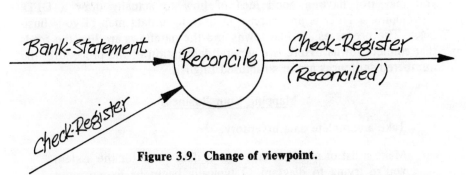

Figure 3.9. Change of viewpoint.

In a *change of organization*, the output data are the same as the input data. However, the organization of the data has changed. Change of organization includes processes such as formatting and sorting. The output of this type of process may or may not be considered to be a different dataflow. In the example of Figure 3.10, Sales-Report would be entered in the dictionary as a new dataflow, possibly with a mock-up of the report. If the process were to sort sales data, you could consider the output to be a different dataflow from the input, or it could be shown as Sales-Data (Sorted).

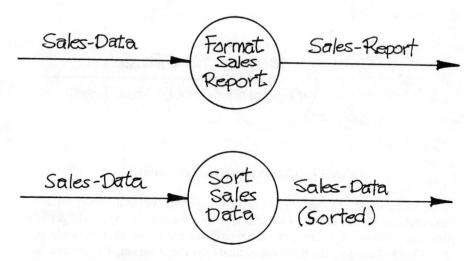

Figure 3.10. Change of organization example.

3.4 Drawing DFDs

Even with the preceding description of DFD rules and guidelines, you may not have a good idea of how to actually draw a DFD. Developing a DFD is an exercise in drawing a data map of your business: The processes are like towns and the dataflows are like the roads that connect towns. Here is a general description of the procedure; the numbered sentences are in structured English.

Mapping Your Business

1. Take a complete data inventory.

   Make a list of all input and output data items for the system you're trying to diagram. I typically begin by listing input dataflows on the left side of the page and output dataflows on the right. This is a completely arbitrary convention that works well for me. Define each data item in the project dictionary.

2.   Repeat the following two steps until all data have been mapped:

    2.1   Choose *one* piece of data.

    2.2   Using DFD notation, map its processing until you can't go further.

The purpose of this procedure is to connect inputs with their corresponding outputs. To avoid being overwhelmed by detail, you proceed by mapping one item of data at a time, following the data item through its transformations and diagramming the processes that transform it and the new dataflows that emerge from these processes. It doesn't really matter which dataflow you choose first. Again arbitrarily, I usually begin with the inputs. If you manage to trace the processing of your one piece of data all the way through to an output, that's great. However, it's more likely either that you will get stuck before coming to an output or that a new output will emerge.

3.   Interconnect the pieces.

At this point, you probably have several unconnected pieces of data flow diagram based on having processed individual inputs or outputs. The remaining task is to interconnect these pieces by adding dataflows, indicating further processing, and adding sources and sinks where they are needed. Instead of tracing a dataflow as in step 2, your focus now is to ensure that each process has all the inputs and outputs it needs to perform its function. If a particular process is incomplete, look around the diagram to find a dataflow that this process either uses or produces. In most systems, all of the data ends up being interrelated in some way, and assuring that every process has all the inputs and outputs it needs tends to reveal this wholeness.

Figures 3.11 through 3.13 show a worked-out example of part of a business called CIS, Inc., that receives contracts and course registrations, and processes them. I've used five steps to build the total diagram, one step for each input, much as one actually does in practice. Applying the first step of the mapping produces the list of data items below; this list is all the data coming into or going out of the system. There are, of course, more data for the entire business, but for this system, I have identified these five only.

Inputs	Outputs
Contract	Contract (Reviewed)
Invoice	Cashflow-Projection
Registration	

For the repetitive procedure required by Step 2, we begin working with the Contract input. After noting on the DFD that the contract is signed, we realize that it is actually used for another purpose and not merely stored. In Figure 3.11, we include this function, which is to estimate the date that payment will be received and to produce certain Cashflow-Data in the process. The Cashflow-Data is used to update a Cashflow-Projection, whose results are stored in a Cashflow-File.

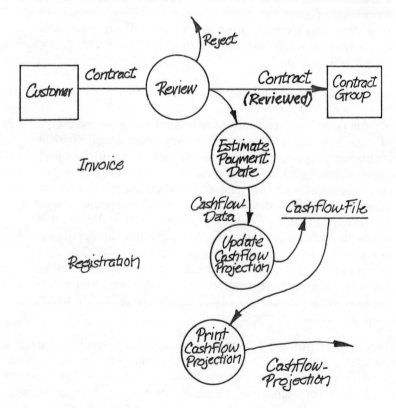

Figure 3.11. Step 2: Mapping the Contract input.

Since Cashflow-Data and Cashflow-File were not on our original list of inputs and outputs, they have no definition in the project dictionary. A very important part of the DFD drawing process is to add to the project dictionary every new dataflow, file, or process as it emerges on the diagram. Hence, we add a definition for Cashflow-Data in Figure 3.11. To be complete, we should add an entry for Cashflow-File as well.

This mapping procedure usually reveals inputs and outputs not included in the original list, because it is almost impossible to list all inputs and outputs ahead of time. Continuing work on this same data path reveals that the new Cashflow-File itself requires further processing. In this case, it generates Cashflow-Projection, one of the outputs we did expect.

We have now completed Step 2 of the mapping procedure for the Contract input. We return to Step 2.1, select the Invoice input, and track its progress, as illustrated by Figure 3.12.

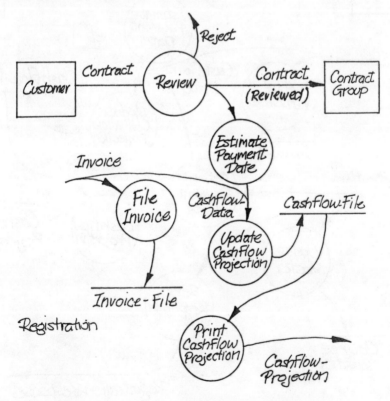

Figure 3.12. Step 2: Mapping the Invoice input.

In isolation, our processing of Invoice might consist simply of filing the Invoice in the unanticipated Invoice-File. However, we may notice that the Cashflow-Projection requires Cashflow-Data from Invoice as well as from Contract; we can show this as a connection with the original Contract processing part of our DFD.

By doing this, we have digressed into Step 3 of the mapping procedure. There is no reason for not following this digression, because it is important to make all connections that you notice *as soon as you notice them*. Otherwise, they may be overlooked.

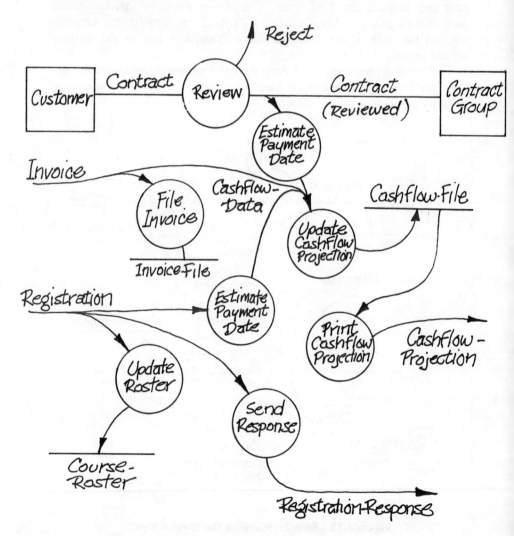

Figure 3.13. Step 2: Mapping the Registration input.

Returning again to Step 2.1, we begin to work with Registration, as shown in Figure 3.13. Following this input reveals a new file and a new output as well: Course-Roster and Registration-Response. It also reveals a connection with the Contract and Invoice processing by means of Cashflow-Data produced by Registration.

Step 2 of the mapping procedure tells us to look now at all of the outputs on the diagram to ensure that they require no further processing. In the DFD of Figure 3.13, no further processing is required.

A review of every process in the diagram as required by Step 3 reveals that they all have the necessary inputs and outputs; no further interconnecting need be done. The diagram is finished and ready for a walkthrough.

3.5 An exercise

I include the following exercise with one of its solutions in case you wish to polish your DFD drawing skills.

The Number One Beverage Mart is a cash-and-carry business run by Sid and Arnie. All transactions are in cash, whether in the form of payment from customers or payment to suppliers for shipments.

Arnie is the boss, so he takes care of all the complicated processing, like checking all the supplies that come into the store and running the cash register. When a customer comes to the check-out area, Arnie takes the money, gives change, and updates his list of what's been bought.

New stock comes from a supplier. If the invoice matches a purchase order, Arnie tells Sid to pay the driver, and he marks the stock list in his pocket to show how much came in and where it's to be kept. When stock is moved within the store, he must also change his list.

Sid organizes the stock on the shelves, and lets Arnie know when they're low on an item. Sometimes, he gets tired of where things are, so he rearranges the shelves and lets Arnie know about it. Sid also puts away new supplies.

When Arnie orders from a supplier, he has to file a copy of the purchase order.

When a customer leaves one of the store's shopping carts in the parking lot, Sid retrieves the cart so that it will be there for the next customer.

Draw your own DFD to represent the Number One Beverage Mart's business according to this description. This is a simple but realistic exercise, which illustrates most of the issues discussed so far. When doing this exercise, be sure to diagram it on paper rather than just thinking or talking about the best way to do it. Don't be discouraged if your first attempt at drawing the diagram doesn't produce the results you want. In classes and on real projects, the teams that do something imperfect at the outset instead of waiting for the perfect solution invariably finish first and have better solutions to show for it.

When you have finished, walk through the diagram, criticizing your own work based on the answers to the following questions:

☐ Is there a file or a process that is a source or a sink?

A file or process with only inputs (a sink) would seem to be useless, since its contents are never accessed. Conversely, having a file or process with only outputs (a source) brings into question where the information came from originally.

☐ Is there a complex interface between processes?

Processes should be drawn to perform a single function. If a process is doing one function only, then its interface with other processes is likely to be fairly simple. A complex interface often suggests that a process is doing multiple functions.

Multiple function processes violate a basic principle of structured systems; namely, any process or module is to perform one and only one function. The reason for this principle is completely pragmatic: Experience has shown repeatedly that the most understandable and highly maintainable systems have predominantly single-function processes.

☐ Has an alias been introduced?

An alias is a new name for something that has been named already. Aliases are the bane of most project dictionaries, particularly when two different analysts are working with the same data, because they may easily use different names for the same item.

Aliases make the specification difficult to maintain. If a change is made in the definition of a particular item of data, the change may go unnoticed in places where the same item is referred to by an alias. Most projects devote considerable attention to detecting and documenting aliases.

☐ Does the DFD observe the six principles described at the beginning of this chapter?

If your colleagues are familiar with drawing DFDs, you may wish to walk through your work with them. One possible solution of the DFD drawing exercise is shown in Figure 3.14.*

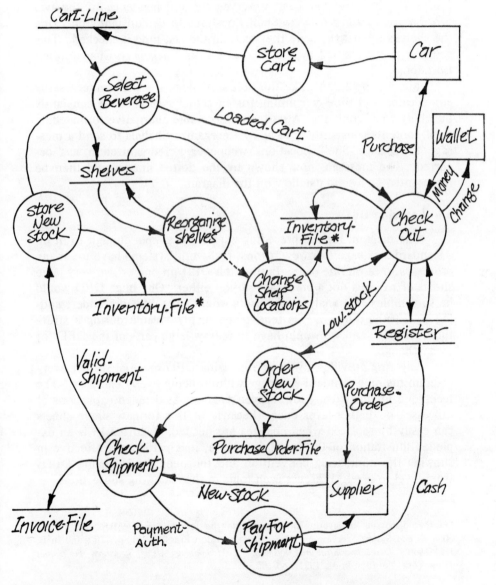

Figure 3.14. The Number One Beverage Mart: DFD solution.

*An asterisk next to each of two files indicates that the files are one and the same; the file is shown in two separate places to avoid a tangle of dataflows.

One notation in the solution needs to be clarified — namely, the dotted dataflow between Reorganize Shelves and Change Shelf Locations. The dotted line is meant to indicate an alternative solution; it is *not* meant to introduce dotted dataflows as part of the DFD notation.

The problem for which I have provided the two solutions is, How does Change Shelf Locations know when the shelves have been reorganized? The way that best preserves the independence of the two processes is to allow Change Shelf Locations to be constantly checking the shelves against the state they were in the last time it checked. This solution is represented by the solid line from Shelves to Change Shelf Locations.

Many people don't like this solution, since it seems unnecessarily complicated and time-consuming for an actual system to be constantly matching shelf contents. A perfectly acceptable alternative to matching shelf contents constantly is to allow Reorganize Shelves to send a message to Change Shelf Locations whenever a reorganization has occurred. The message, now shown by the dotted line, would then be represented by a solid dataflow on the diagram.

3.6 Layering DFDs

The diagram for the preceding exercise is simple enough to fit on a standard-size page. However, most real-world systems have too many processes to fit on one page. Putting the DFD on one or two very large sheets of paper is not a practical solution either: One huge DFD would be so complex that analysts and users would have difficulty understanding it. Furthermore, DFDs tend to be highly volatile during a structured analysis, and we would have to redraw large parts of the DFD for every change.

Layering provides a way of organizing DFD material so that every diagram fits on a standard-size page without being overly complex.* The technique involves using lower-layer diagrams as detailed explosions of processes on higher-layer ones. Because of this format, single sheets can easily be replaced when changes are needed. Figure 3.15 is an exploded illustration of the layering process; it is particularly effective in showing the numbering convention and the need for balancing DFDs from level to level. I discuss each topic in the following subsections.

---

*Further discussion of layering or leveling may be found in T. DeMarco's *Structured Analysis and System Specification* (New York: Yourdon Press, 1979), p. 71ff.; and in B. Dickinson's *Developing Structured Systems: A Methodology Using Structured Techniques* (New York: Yourdon Press, 1981), pp. 9ff.

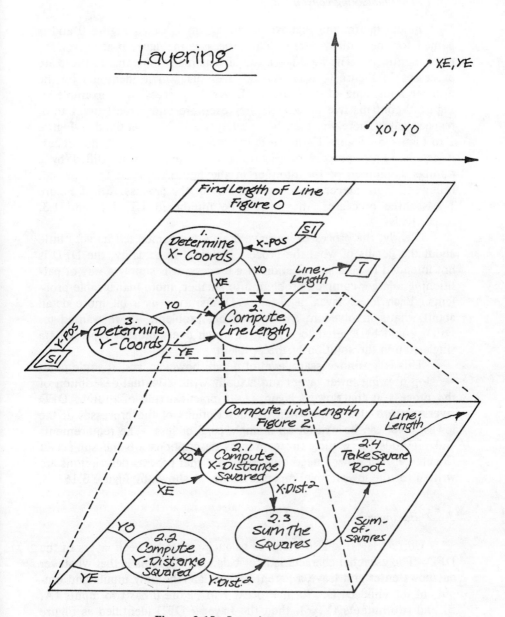

Figure 3.15. Layering example.

3.6.1 The numbering convention

In the figure, the highest-layer diagram is called Figure 0 and is named for the entire system. The processes in Figure 0 are given integer identifiers. The next layer contains as many diagrams as there are processes in Figure 0; each second-layer diagram is identified by the number and name of a Figure 0 (Layer 1) process. For example, if Figure 0 contains five processes, they each are numbered from 1 to 5, respectively. There will then be five Layer 2 DFDs identified as Figure 1 to Figure 5. Figure 1's name is the same as the name of the process it details. Each process on Figure 1 to Figure 5 is identified by a number composed of the number of the figure followed by a period, followed by an integer sequence number for the process. So, if Figure 1 has three processes, they would be numbered 1.1, 1.2, and 1.3, respectively.

Clearly, the processes we have drawn and named tell us very little about the details of what the process is doing. In actuality, the DFD is not intended to be a specification of a process; it is simply a way of partitioning a large, complex problem into smaller, more manageable problems. Each lower layer of a set of DFDs gives us a bit more detail about what's involved in solving the big problem. If we wanted to, DFDs could be layered to a point at which every process represents a single step in the solution of the problem.

This is an unnecessary level of detail, however, and at some point we stop drawing lower layers and actually write a textual description of the process at that lowest layer. As a practical rule of thumb, DFD layering stops at a point when the descriptions of the processes at the lowest level can be written on a single page or less. The requirements and methods for writing those process descriptions are the subject of Chapter 4. For now, I need only point out that process descriptions are written for the lowest-level processes only, as shown by Figure 3.16.

3.6.2 Balancing

Correct layering also involves balancing data between layers of the DFD. The essential characteristic of balanced diagrams is that whatever dataflows enter and leave a parent process are the only inputs and outputs of the child DFD. So, if Process 1 in Figure 0 has two inputs (A, B) and two outputs (Y, Z), then the Layer 2 DFD identified as Figure 1 will have only A and B as inputs and only Y and Z as outputs.

In actuality, there are three types of balancing: visual balancing, used when both the parent and child diagrams use the same dataflow names; dictionary balancing, used when the child diagram contains dataflows that are the constituents of the parent dataflows; and file balancing.

Visual balancing, shown in Figure 3.17, is the easiest to apply since there is a one-to-one correspondence between names at a particular level and those at the level below it.

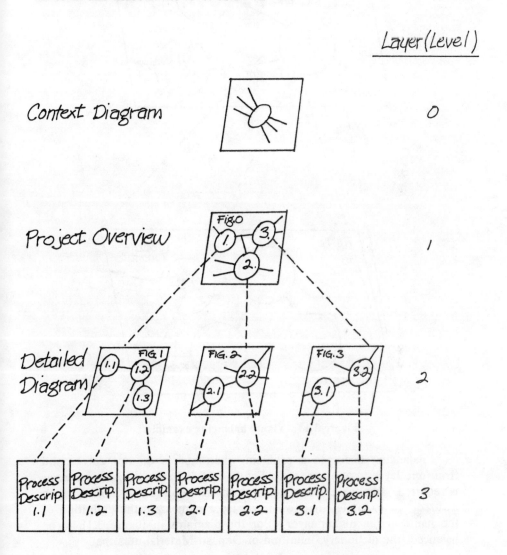

Figure 3.16. DFD set with process descriptions.

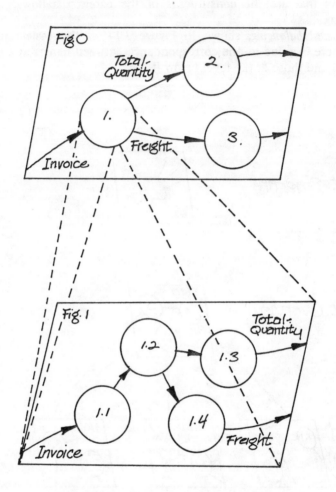

Figure 3.17. Visual balancing example.

Balancing becomes a problem when names do not correspond from one layer to another, as in Figure 3.18, where *dictionary balancing* is required. In such a case, one must check the project dictionary to be assured, for example, that two lower-layer names are the definition of the name at the higher layer. For the diagrams in Figure 3.18 to be balanced, the dictionary definition of Deposit-Material must be

Deposit-Material = Cash + Deposit-Ticket

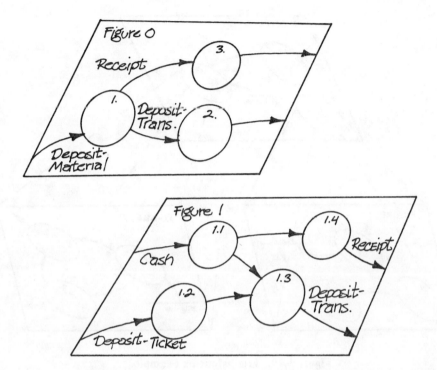

Figure 3.18. Dictionary balancing example.

File balancing, as shown in Figure 3.19, is a slightly different subject. The rule regarding file balancing between DFDs is that a file appears at the highest layer where it is shared by two or more processes. At that level, all accesses to the file are shown. A file must also appear on the child diagram of all processes that use the file. Observe that File A, which is both updated and accessed in Figure 0, appears only updated or only accessed at the lower level. Although files should not have only inputs or only outputs, it's okay to have File A appear as a source or a sink at the lower level as long as it is used both ways at the higher level.

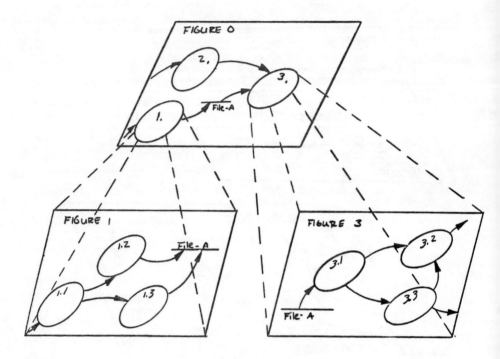

Figure 3.19. File balancing example.

Although the diagram in Figure 3.16 is neatly layered to the same depth throughout, such symmetry is not a requirement of the method. Processes in the same layer can differ in complexity and therefore require differing numbers of layers below them. The partitioning in Figure 0, at least through to current logical diagrams, is often determined more by political expediency than by a desire to equalize the complexity of processes.

In a Figure 0 diagram, which shows the processes Sales Department, Manufacturing Department, and so on, there could be a process called Produce General Manager's Report. Even though this last process is trivial compared with the others, it may be important to the general manager (who will review nothing but Figure 0) to see that such a report is included. In another case, it could be that a very complicated process is virtually unknown and cannot be diagrammed in more detail now, yet it is important to include it for later analysis.

Structured analysis is excellent for both these situations. It allows varying detail at any level and also allows large pieces of the system to remain in the specification, unanalyzed indefinitely, even while much of the rest of the system goes into design and implementation.

To test your mastery of DFDs, try the following DFD quiz, which asks you to find the balancing and numbering errors in a two-level set of DFDs.

Parent

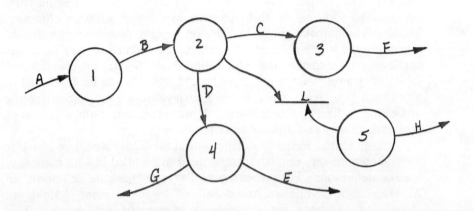

Child 2

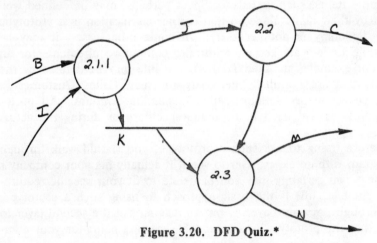

Figure 3.20. DFD Quiz.*

---

*Answers appear at the end of the chapter.

3.7 The prototype system

In the real world, DFDs tend to be much more complex than the simple examples given here or in courses on structured analysis. Still, the basic principles are sound and can be applied step by step to build a structured specification for an actual project.

A way to help simplify the development of a complex system is to use prototypes. Many business processes are basically the same from company to company or from division to division within a company. Thus, it could make sense to develop certain prototype new logical specifications, which need only be refined and tailored for any particular application by incorporating information from the current physical and logical diagrams. Such a prototype would probably not be developed to more than two layers, since below that level much application-specific processing is likely to be present. It would include both a prototype project dictionary and process descriptions.

Many entries in the prototype project dictionary would be blank or include commentary only and would need to be filled in with company-specific definitions. For an example of a prototype data definition, an All-Data-Suspense-File might be defined by a comment, "Holds all records in suspense for subsequent adjustment processing." This definition recognizes the universal need for holding erroneous input for later correction, but declines to put any specific content or format restrictions on the file.

Some items, such as Balance-Sheet perhaps, may be defined well enough by their name alone so that further clarification in a prototype project dictionary is not necessary. In some other cases, it may be worthwhile to indicate certain minimum content requirements for an item. For example, an Aged-Trial-Balance-File may be defined by the elements that are minimally necessary for such a file: Customer-#, Invoice-Date, Invoice-Amount, and Outstanding-Amount. All prototype definitions will need to be made specific later during the actual project.

Before trying to use such a prototype, you should walk through the diagram with an expert user to see if it actually fits your company's situation. You certainly may add or delete to fit your specific requirements. In fact, this is the basic approach to using such a prototype: Walk through not only Layer 1, but all diagrams at the second layer to ensure that the prototype is a reasonable starting point for your company.

Having such a prototype does not obviate the need for current physical and logical diagrams; they are necessary. The prototype new logical diagram is a guide for turning your current system into a system that many years of experience have shown to be best for managing the particular piece of the business under analysis.

It is only after the current system has been documented and the applicability of the prototype verified by company experts that refinement of the prototype should be undertaken.

3.8 Summary

The data flow diagram is the primary tool of structured analysis for documenting the processing of data in order to develop a system that meets the user's needs. This chapter has examined in some depth the DFD technique for mapping the processing of real data. We also have looked at the layering technique for organizing a set of DFDs and have proposed the use of a prototype set of DFDs as a starting point for a project.

Having discussed both data and DFDs, we are in a position to learn about another major piece of the structured analysis repertoire of tools, the process and techniques for describing it.

Answers to DFD Quiz

1. I appears as an input on the child diagram but does not appear on the parent diagram.

2. Similarly, M and N appear as outputs from the child diagram but are not shown on the parent.

    If I, M, and N are valid inputs and outputs on the child, then the parent should be changed to include them.

3. Process 2 writes to File L, but File L does not appear on the child.

4. File L is only written to. Although this may be true for a particular system, it is suspect and should be raised as a question for the user.

5. The child's numbering convention is wrong. Process 2.1.1 should be numbered 2.1.

4

DFD Process Descriptions

In developing a set of layered DFDs, no processing is actually specified until the bottom layer is reached. Until that point, the layering serves only to break a large and unwieldy problem into smaller, more manageable pieces. The entire system could actually be specified by connecting all of the bottom layer DFDs; the layering procedure is done to make reviewing the work and constructing the system convenient. This chapter considers how processes are named and described so that they can later be turned into automated processes.

4.1 Naming processes

The data flow diagram is like a snapshot of a group of people, some of whom you may recognize, some you may remember vaguely, and others you may not know at all. In order to identify the participants, you need a description of who they are and what they're doing. Like snapshots, data flow diagrams are images of change, *not* descriptions of change.

The intention of process naming is to find a name that is meaningful enough to give the reader a pretty good idea of what the process does without giving the impression that the name tells everything. For example, "Update Master File Using the Transaction File Being Sure to Ignore Duplicate Transactions" is obviously too detailed. It's nice if process names completely describe the process, but this is unusual. In the Gane and Sarson notation, the rounded-rectangle process boxes are often drawn large enough for a lengthy process name to be used.* This has the disadvantage that you may think you understand what policy the process describes when, in fact, there are many subtleties hidden behind the name. At the other extreme, "Update" is really too brief a name for a process to update a master file, since it gives no indication of what's being updated.

Keep process names short, but meaningful. Using a single-verb, single-direct-object name helps to ensure that a process, and not data, is described. Be sure, however, that the verb and object combination accurately encompasses what the process is to do.

4.2 Qualities of a meaningful process description

Specification of a process begins by naming it. However, it is in the description of the process that the analyst must pay full attention to satisfying the goal of making a complete, unambiguous, and nonredundant process specification. Clearly, not just any description will do. Its meaning must be precise, which means, among other things, that it must be tied directly to the project dictionary for the system.

According to Wilks, to be meaningful is to have one and only one interpretation with respect to some dictionary.† For our purposes, the dictionary is the project dictionary. All nouns in the process description must be defined in the project dictionary.

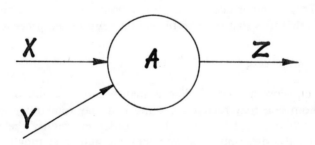

Figure 4.1. A process in need of a description.

---

*C. Gane and T. Sarson, *Structured Systems Analysis: Tools & Techniques* (New York: Improved System Technologies, 1977).
†Y. Wilks, *Meaning and the Machine Analysis of Language* (London: Routledge & Kegan-Paul, 1972).

If a project description has one and only one interpretation with respect to a project dictionary, it will satisfy three criteria for a meaningful process description: It will be complete, unambiguous, and nonredundant. In Figure 4.1, a meaningful description of A is one that describes completely and unambiguously the changing of X and Y into Z (and nothing else), and whose terms X, Y, and Z are defined in the project dictionary. The three characteristics of a meaningful process description are discussed below.

4.2.1 Completeness

For a process description to be meaningful, the user must recognize the description as being a complete and accurate description of the policy in question. The analyst can ensure completeness fairly easily by considering whether all data on the diagram are dealt with. Sometimes, new dataflows are discovered as a result of writing the process description, and these must be added to both the DFDs and the project dictionary.

For example, if the DFD has an Update Master File process with the outputs Master-File and Transaction-Suspense, it is not enough to describe the updating of the master file only. The process description must also specify the policy that causes a Transaction-Suspense item to be output. The fact that the completeness of the description can often be guaranteed by ensuring that all inputs and outputs are described emphasizes the importance of the analyst's working closely with the user to determine what all of those inputs and outputs are.

4.2.2 Ambiguity

In addition to being complete, the process descriptions must be unambiguous. Ambiguity is the spice that makes our natural English language exciting and dynamic. In a systems specification, however, ambiguity is synonymous with catastrophe, since designers can misinterpret the process description and design the wrong function.

Misunderstanding can result from two types of ambiguity that can creep into a process description: ambiguity of word sense ("he needs a jack"), and ambiguity of construction ("they are flying planes").

There are numerous examples of simple sentences that are impossible to clarify without further information. "I saw the man on the hill with a telescope" has two immediate interpretations:

- I looked through a telescope and saw the man on the hill.
- I saw the man who was on the hill and who had a telescope.

In another example, "They are flying planes" has at least three possible meanings:

- They (certain people) are piloting airplanes.
- They (certain people) are flying model airplanes.
- They (certain objects) are airplanes that fly.

The point is that most users, in fact most people, are not attuned to detecting ambiguities in the things they say. For this reason, the analyst must listen carefully to a user's description of a particular business policy, attentive to all possible interpretations of what the user is saying.

4.2.3 Redundancy

Describing a process redundantly means saying the same thing more than once; it is the least serious defect of a process description. The problem is that redundancy often leads to confusion, since the same thing said twice is usually said differently each time.

If in one part of the policy I state "increase salaries by ten percent" and in another place "new salaries are one hundred and ten percent of the old salaries," it is not immediately clear that I've said the same thing twice. In such a case, the analyst and user need to work together to unify the redundant statements.

4.3 Structured English

Structured analysis offers an aid to writing good process descriptions: Structured English uses the syntax of everyday English but restricts itself to simple sentence constructions and a few necessary but sufficient logical constructs. Structured English provides a medium for capturing completely, unambiguously, and nonredundantly the meaning of a user's description.

Although the style of structured English varies widely from project to project, the logical constructs on which it is based remain the same. These necessary but sufficient constructs also happen to be the same constructs that underlie the discipline of structured programming:

- the PROCESS construct, in which a process is done and control passes directly to the next step; for example,

    − Format the Daily-Audit-Report
    − Change the Daily-Activity-Status to "Reported"
    − Validate Customer-Name from Customer-File
    − Get a Work-Order from the Work-Order-File

- the CONDITIONAL or IF-THEN-ELSE construct, in which the next step is determined by some condition in the program; for example,

IF there are more than four Active-Work-Orders
THEN
> Send a More-Than-Four message

OTHERWISE (< 4)
> Send a Work-Order-Number

- the LOOP, which allows repeated execution of certain steps until or while some condition exists; for example,

1.   REPEAT the following for each Employee

    1.1   Get the Employment-History

    1.2   Enter New-Salary

A major advantage of using structured English is that the process description flows from the top to the bottom of the page, even while the various constructs are nested to any required depth. Remember that the best process descriptions fit on one page or less, but usually not on less than half a page.

Another advantage is that structured English converts easily and naturally into a structured program because it uses the same constructs. I have a friend who taught structured programming at a major university; his method of grading student's programs was unique. He would tack the program on the wall and throw a dart at the listing. Wherever the dart landed, the student had thirty seconds to tell him exactly under what conditions that statement would be executed; one letter grade was removed for every five seconds over that thirty-second limit. The point is that a programmer's productivity is heavily dependent on the ability to discover quickly where and why a program has failed. Structured programming allows the programmer to do this and using structured English makes structured programming easy.

Following are two examples of structured English that show the same process described in two different styles. The first example shows an abbreviated, codelike style with numbering and indentation to emphasize the underlying logic.

Process 1.3 — Increase Salaries

1. For each Employee in the Personnel-File
   - 1.1   If Years-Employed > 10
     - 1.1.1   Update Employee-Record:
       Set New-Salary to Salary × Years-Employed × 11%
     - Otherwise (Years-Employed ≤ 10)
     - 1.1.2   Set New-Salary to Salary × 105%
   - 1.2   Place New-Salary in New-Salary-File
   - 1.3   Add New-Salary to Total-Salary

2. If Total-Salary < 1,000,000
   - 2.1   Print Salary-Summary
   - 2.2   Update Salary-File
   - Otherwise (Total-Salary ≥ 1,000,000)
   - 2.3   Print Over-Budget-Report
   - 2.4   Delete New-Salary-File

The second style represents the other end of the spectrum, a flowing narrative. Line numbers from style 1 are included to show the logical equivalence of these two descriptions.

Process 1.3 — Increase Salaries

Go through the personnel file, one employee at a time (1), and ask if that person has been with the company for more than ten years (1.1). If so, change the salary by multiplying it by the number of years with the company, and that figure by 11% (1.1.1). This is the new salary. It is put into the new salary file (1.2). If the employee has been with the company ten years or less, we simply increase the salary by 5% to form the new salary (1.1.2). In either case, keep a running total of the new salaries (1.3).

If the total salary for all employees is less than $1,000,000 (2), print a salary summary (2.1) and update the salary file (2.2). Otherwise, put out an over-budget report (2.3), and erase all the new salaries (2.4).

Although codelike structured English as in the first example is easiest for an analyst to understand, end users generally hate it. From the point of view of logical rigor, there is no reason why a structured process description can't use a fluent, conversational style. Such a style satisfies the important goal of structured English — namely, to preserve the logical sequence of statements using process, conditional, and loop constructs only.

The difficulty with a narrative style is that logical inconsistencies can hide more easily in the description. Since the description doesn't look like the code, the separation of constructs is somewhat less obvious. The systems analyst must simply be more attentive in order to produce an accurate structured English description in a narrative style. In many cases, the easiest approach is to write codelike structured English and then translate it into a more narrative style.

If you wish to try writing structured English, here is an exercise, with a solution, that uses a one-process data flow diagram, several data dictionary definitions, and an unstructured description of its function. The objective is to write the structured English equivalent of this description. First, read the unstructured description, referring to the DFD, then write a structured English description. When you have finished, compare your version of structured English with my suggested solution.

4.3.1 Structured English exercise

Process 6.4 — Process Credit Card Transaction
(unstructured English)

The purpose of this process is to decide whether to send a customer a mild dunning letter, the ultimate dunning letter, or no letter at all. If a customer is over his credit limit by under $100 after all transactions, send a mild dunning letter. But if the customer is more than $100 over his credit limit, send him the ultimate dunning letter, and place him on the hot credit list.

When the customer makes a payment, increase his available credit (in the account authorization file) by whatever amount he paid. Naturally, if his account is overdrawn, reduce the amount of the overdraft before increasing the available credit. Always return the updated account authorization file record to the file.

Authorization requests can only decrease the available credit amount, but not below zero, and may result in increasing the overdraft amount.

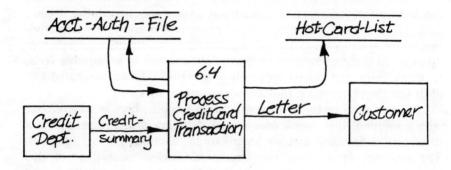

Figure 4.2. DFD for Process Credit Card Transaction.

Acct-Auth-File   =   {Credit-Card-Number + Available-Credit + Overdraft}

Credit-Summary   =   Credit-Card-Number + {Credit-Trans}

Credit-Trans   =   Trans-Type + Trans-Amount + Trans-Date

Hot-Card-List   =   {Credit-Card-Number}

Letter   = $\begin{bmatrix} \text{Mild-Dunning-Letter} \\ \text{Ultimate-Dunning-Letter} \end{bmatrix}$

Trans-Type   = $\begin{bmatrix} \text{Payment} \\ \text{Auth-Req} \end{bmatrix}$

I use the DFD in this example to introduce an alternative notation for DFDs, that of Gane and Sarson.* Several other notations are in
use, including one that uses ovals instead of circles or rounded rectan-
gles; but the differences in the approaches to structured analysis are
insignificant.

---

*C. Gane and T. Sarson, op. cit.

4.3.2 Structured English solution

A possible solution appears below.

Process 6.4 — Process Credit Card Transaction

1. For each Credit-Trans in the Credit-Summary

    1.1 Access Acct-Auth-File using Credit-Card-Number as a key

    1.2 Depending on the Trans-Type:

        1.2.1 (Trans-Type is Payment)
            If Overdraft = 0
                Increase Available-Credit by Trans-Amount
            Else (Overdraft > 0)
                If Overdraft $\geq$ Trans-Amount
                    Reduce Overdraft by Trans-Amount
                Else (Overdraft < Trans-Amount)
                    Increase Available-Credit by Trans-Amount
                    minus Overdraft
                    Set Overdraft to 0

        1.2.2 (Trans-Type is Auth-Req)
            If Available-Credit $\geq$ Trans-Amount
                Decrease Available-Credit by Trans-Amount
            Else (Available-Credit < Trans-Amount)
                Increase Overdraft by Trans-Amount
                minus Available-Credit
                Set Available-Credit to 0

2. If Available-Credit = 0

    2.1 If Overdraft $\geq$ 100

        2.1.1 Send Ultimate-Dunning-Letter

        2.1.2 Place Credit-Card-Number on Hot-Card-List

        Else (Overdraft < 100)

        2.1.3 Send Mild-Dunning-Letter to Customer

    Else (Available-Credit > 0)

    2.2 Ignore Customer

3. Replace Acct-Auth-File record

4.4 Decision tables and decision trees

Decision tables and decision trees, which were popular in the 1960s, are alternatives to structured English for the specification of processes. These tabular and graphic techniques for specifying policy are particularly useful for depicting multiple interrelated conditions and for detecting incomplete specification.

The procedure for developing a decision table is straightforward. First, list all of the logical conditions that apply to the problem. Next, list all possible actions that can result from various combinations of the values those conditions can take on.

Third, draw a table with enough columns to include all possible logical combinations of conditions. The number of columns required is determined by the number of different values for each condition. In the abstract example of Table 4.1, each of the two conditions can have two values, True and False, so four columns are required. The final step is to move through the table, column by column, and mark the actions to be taken in response to each combination of conditions.

Figure 4.4 shows a decision tree that depicts the same abstract example. The two techniques differ only in that the tree follows a direction at a right angle to the decision table. In practice, I find that users tend to prefer the decision tree because the logic can be read from left to right.

Table 4.1
Abstract Example of a Decision Table

Process Name				
Condition 1	T	T	F	F
Condition 2	T	F	T	F
Action 1		X	?	X
Action 2	X	X		X
Action 3				X

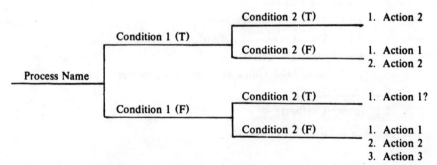

Figure 4.3. Abstract example of a decision tree.

In one place, a question mark has been entered. This means that it is difficult (or impossible) to tell from the description what action should be taken. This situation occurs frequently. Seldom if ever do narrative descriptions cover all possibilities. Wherever there are questions about what action should be taken the user has the final word.

I offer the following Restaurant Policy as an exercise to test your skills at developing a decision table or a decision tree. After reading the Restaurant Policy description, try to represent its logical conditions as either a decision table or a decision tree. A solution for each technique follows the exercise.

4.4.1 Decision tree and table exercise

Restaurant Policy

I often go to a restaurant on the spur of the moment and I am easily upset if I am not seated immediately; here's the way I feel about it.

If the wait isn't more than about ten minutes, I just stand in the lobby, although I don't like to wait at all. If the wait is longer than ten minutes, I go to the lounge. To wait more than half an hour is ridiculous when the restaurant has no lounge; I leave and get a pizza, unless it's a really good restaurant, with a meal costing more than $25. That's worth the wait. Still, I usually gripe to the manager.

Having to wait more than ten minutes in a restaurant without a lounge when a meal costs less than $10 sends me off to a fast-food place. In any case, if I can get a drink in the lounge, I'll wait all night for a meal in any restaurant.

4.4.2 Exercise solutions

Table 4.2
Restaurant Policy Expressed as a Decision Table

Average price	<10	<10	<10	<10	<10	<10	10–25	10–25	10–25	10–25	10–25	10–25	>25	>25	>25	>25	>25	>25
Wait time	<10	<10	10–30	10–30	>30	>30	<10	<10	10–30	10–30	>30	>30	<10	<10	10–30	10–30	>30	>30
Lounge	T	F	T	F	T	F	T	F	T	F	T	F	T	F	T	F	T	F
Wait impatiently	X	X					X	X		X			X	X		X		X
Go to lounge			X		X				X		X				X		X	
Fast food				X		X						X						
Complain to manager						?						?						X

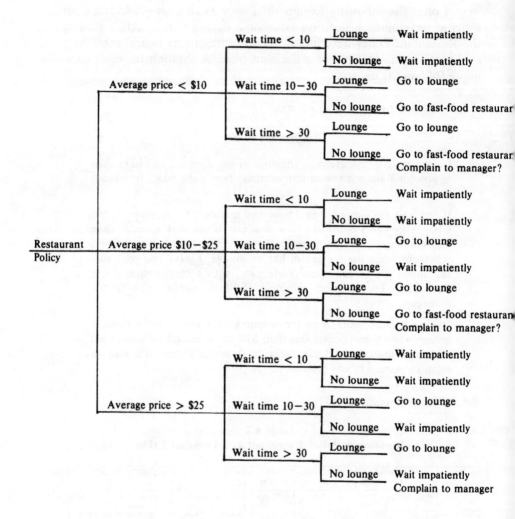

Figure 4.4. Restaurant policy expressed as a decision tree.

Remember that the structured English, decision table, and decision tree approaches are only suggestions for describing business policy. Structured English is generally the method of choice in most structured projects. However, decision tables and decision trees are useful for processes with many interrelated conditions, as said before.

4.4.3 An alternative method

For certain processes, some other method not described here may be more applicable. Any complete, unambiguous, nonredundant method is acceptable. One alternative is the price list in Figure 4.5 for Delaware Valley Office Products. The DFD in Figure 4.6 illustrates the Determine Price Per Copy process.

BASE PRICE PER SINGLE-SIDED COPY

		Number of same size originals						
		1-4	5-10	11-20	21-36	37-60	61-99	100+
	1	.100	.100	.100	.100	.095	.090	.085
	2	.100	.100	.100	.095	.088	.083	.079
*	3	.100	.100	.095	.091	.084	.077	.074
	4	.100	.100	.093	.088	.081	.075	.071
*	5	.100	.100	.091	.086	.078	.074	.069
	6	.100	.096	.089	.083	.077	.072	.067
*	7	.100	.094	.088	.082	.075	.069	.065
	8	.100	.093	.087	.080	.074	.068	.064
*	9	.100	.092	.086	.079	.073	.067	.063
	10-15	.098	.091	.084	.077	.071	.066	.062
Number	16-20	.090	.083	.077	.072	.064	.060	.056
	21-25	.085	.078	.071	.066	.060	.055	.052
of	26-30	.080	.072	.066	.063	.057	.053	.048
	31-35	.075	.068	.063	.059	.054	.050	.046
copies	36-40	.069	.065	.060	.056	.052	.048	.044
	41-45	.066	.062	.058	.054	.050	.046	.043
from	46-50	.063	.059	.056	.052	.048	.045	.041
	51-60	.061	.057	.053	.049	.046	.044	.039
each	61-70	.058	.054	.050	.047	.044	.042	.038
	71-80	.055	.052	.049	.046	.042	.040	.037
same	81-90	.053	.050	.047	.044	.040	.038	.035
	91-100	.050	.048	.045	.042	.038	.036	.034
size	101-149	.048	.045	.042	.040	.037	.035	.033
	150-199	.042	.040	.037	.036	.033	.032	.030
original	200-249	.036	.035	.033	.032	.030	.028	.028
	250-299	.033	.032	.030	.029	.028	.027	.026
*	300-399	.030	.029	.028	.027	.026	.025	.025
	400-499	.027	.026	.025	.024	.024	.024	.024
*	500-599	.025	.024	.023	.023	.023	.023	.023
	600-699	.023	.022	.022	.022	.022	.022	.022
*	700 799	.022	.021	.021	.021	.021	.021	.021
	800-899	.021	.020	.020	.020	.020	.020	.020
*	900-999	.020	.019	.019	.019	.019	.019	.019
	1000+	.019	.018	.018	.018	.018	.018	.018

SIZE	PRINTING MEDIUM	PRICE PER PAGE
8½X11	Customers stock*	Base price
"	20 lb. subs. bond, white	Base price
"	20 lb. subs. bond, colors	Base price + .003
"	20 lb. Hammermill colors	Base price + .010
"	20 lb. 25% rag, white	Base price + .012
"	24 lb. subs. bond, white	Base price + .004
"	28 lb. subs. bond, white	Base price + .007
"	110 lb. index, white & colors	Base price + .022
"	33 pressure sensitive labels	Base price + .17
"	Adhesive transfer film	1.25 each
"	Transparency	.75
8½X14	20 lb. subs. bond, white	Base price + .004
11X17	20 lb. subs. bond, white	.25 each

*If compatible with our Xerox equipment

Form courtesy of Delaware Valley Office Products, Media, PA

Figure 4.5. Price list example.

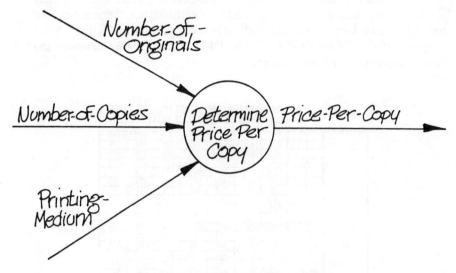

Figure 4.6. DFD for pricing example.

4.5 Structured English and pseudocode

What is the difference between structured English and pseudocode? and, Can one technique be used for both analysis and design? Those questions come up regularly in projects. In this section, I want to compare structured English to pseudocode and show that in some cases a single process description depicted in one or the other form can serve both analysis and design.

The process of design is to turn the what-we-want-to-do goal of structured analysis into the how-we-are-going-to-do-it solution. Therefore, the business policy expressed in structured English during the analysis phase must be turned into step-by-step algorithmic statements of the process a person or a computer must execute to achieve the transformation of input data to output data. Pseudocode is one technique used by structured design to state the algorithm a particular module must execute. Although structured English and pseudocode use identical logical constructs, pseudocode differs from structured English both in its level of detail and in its style. To see this difference, compare the structured English description of Update Master File and the pseudocode description of the same process given below. Figure 4.7 shows a structured flowchart equivalent of the pseudocode; it is equally acceptable as a module description during design. The structured flowchart is also known as a Chapin chart or a Nassi-Shneiderman diagram.

Update Master File
(structured English version)

Depending on which case applies:

1. (transaction matches master)
    Make changes to the master and write it out

2. (transaction > master)
    Write out the master unchanged

3. (transaction < master)
    Show an error

Update Master File
(pseudocode version)

```
Call Get Master
Call Get Transaction

Do while more masters & more transactions
If transaction = master
Then do:  Call Apply Transaction
          Call Put Master
          Call Get Master
          Call Get Transaction          End
Else
If transaction > master
Then do:  Call Put Master
          Call Get Master               End
Else
If transaction < master
Then do:  Call Error
          Call Get Transaction          End
End

Do while more masters
    Call Put Master
    Call Get Master
End

Do while more transactions
    Call Error
    Call Get Transaction
End
```

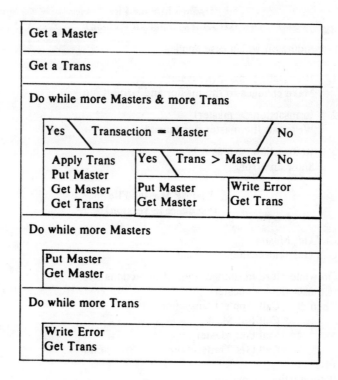

Figure 4.7. Structured flowchart.

The structured English description contains the logic of updating a master file. It is clearly driven by the updating transaction, and even gives a good idea of what to do depending on the relationship between the transaction and master file records. The pseudocode description is definitely codelike and very detailed. One could almost write a statement-for-statement transcription of this into a high-level programming language such as PL/I. That is exactly the point: Structured design makes it fairly easy to turn over to relatively low-level coders the task of actually producing working computer programs.

The level of detail to which pseudocode is written depends partly on who is doing the programming. To give detailed pseudocode to a senior programmer would be an insult, considering the skill accumulated over many years of programming. It is far better to give senior programmers a slight elaboration of the structured English, or possibly just the structured English itself. On the other hand, having detailed pseudocode available can minimize delays in the project in case of the untimely departure of a senior programmer. The method of writing only one description that serves both analysis and design is most appropriate for very small projects in which the analyst, designer, and programmer are likely to be the same person.

Clearly, narrative, high-level structured English and detailed, codelike pseudocode are at opposite ends of a broad spectrum of process description. The style and content of structured English and pseudocode used on a particular project are always a matter of negotiation among the people who are using, analyzing, designing, and programming the system. There are no rigorous rules for making this choice.

4.6 Summary

A study of process descriptions completes our overview of the tools of structured analysis. We have looked at the important considerations in writing process descriptions such as eliminating ambiguity and redundancy. We have also seen some techniques for writing actual process descriptions, including structured English, decision tables, decision trees, and pseudocode. We are now ready to review the project life cycle in the next chapter to see how these tools fit into the scheme of an overall structured project.

5

Structured Analysis and the Project Life Cycle

Having looked closely at the tools of structured analysis, I will now show where to use them during the analysis portion of the life cycle of a structured project. A life cycle diagram, such as that shown in Figure 5.1, indicates the major activities in a project from its inception to its completion. It is drawn as Figure 0 of a set of DFDs. Figure 5.1 is similar to that of DeMarco except that it shows two more activities: database design (Process 3) and systems integration (Process 5).* The analysis-related activities are discussed in the following sections.

5.1 Survey

Every company has its own way of deciding whether to begin a project. Some companies seem to flip a coin or to consult a crystal ball, whereas others choose some equally obscure method, but all companies that are serious about beginning a project should complete a survey or preliminary study (Process 1 of Figure 5.1). The output of this preliminary project planning is called a scope definition, feasibility document, or project overview.

---

*T. DeMarco, *Structured Analysis and System Specification* (New York: Yourdon Press, 1979), pp. 22ff.

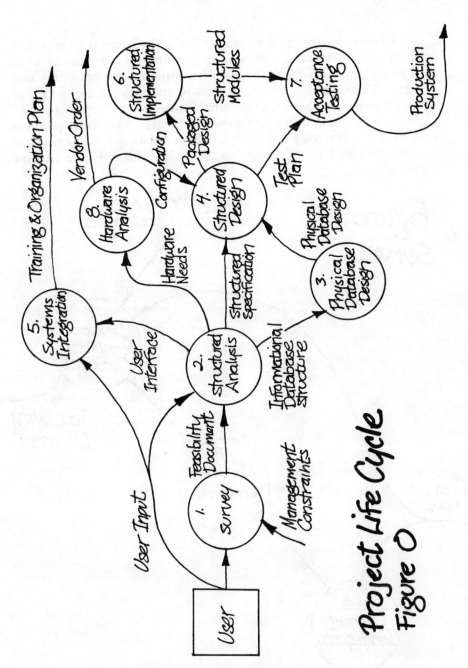

Figure 5.1. The project life cycle.

Whatever its name, the purpose of the document is to provide a general description of the changes in a predetermined business area, and to give an overview of the projected costs and benefits of the new system. This outline of goals and costs summarizes the user's view of the new system and becomes the primary input to structured analysis.

The survey is really a miniature structured analysis, requiring a few days to a few weeks. Figure 5.2 shows a data flow diagram of the survey, Process 1 of the structured life cycle. This is Figure 1 of the DFD set.

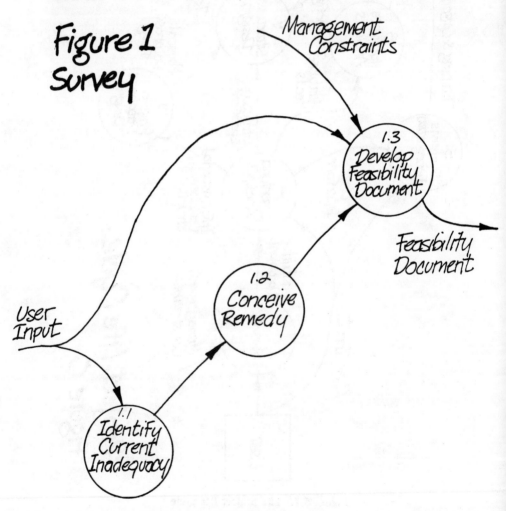

Figure 5.2. Survey (Process 1).

Most traditional feasibility documents I have seen have been long-winded attempts to convince an unwilling manager that a good, though ill-defined idea for a new system was worth funding. The technical content of these documents has been almost always incomplete, ambiguous, and redundant.

As a practical way of getting the analysis off on the right foot, why not use DFDs, probably at a very high level, to describe the changes to be included in the feasibility document? The most frequent reason given for not doing this ("the division manager won't look at DFDs") implies a lack of training. For the structured approach to produce maximum benefits in a company, it is important to train not only systems people, but users and managers as well. However, it is not a crushing blow for the analysis phase to have unstructured inputs.

5.2 Structured analysis

Process 2, the structured analysis phase, uses the results of the survey, together with continuing interviews and reviews with users to develop a structured specification of what the user wants to see in a new system. Figure 5.3 indicates, in DFD form, the details of the structured analysis phase. Developing a structured specification has four steps, which tend to overlap and repeat. These steps are discussed in the following subsections.

5.2.1 Describe the current model

Step 1 in the development of a structured specification is to derive two sets of DFDs that depict the existing system: The first set of DFDs shows the system in all its redundant, implementation-dependent glory, and the second set shows the system after removing all of the implementation-dependent characteristics from the current description of the system. The reason for documenting the current system is simply that we must know ahead of time how our new system is to interface with the rest of the existing environment and what existing functions need to be changed or deleted.

Typically, an existing physical system does not completely meet the needs of the day-to-day running of the business: It has been constrained by technological limitations and by the need to produce a working system in a finite time. Furthermore, because the system has been changed over the years to respond to changing business needs, the system is unplanned and has a patchwork quality. The step of functionalizing existing processes and data removes their constraints and focuses on the business functions that underlie the current system.

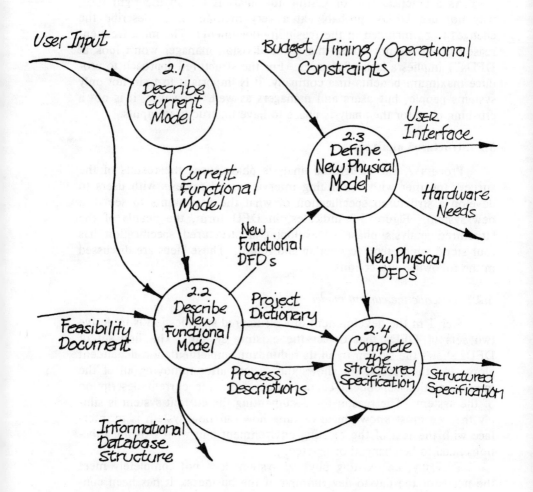

Figure 5.3. Steps in structured analysis (Process 2).

5.2.2 Describe the new functional model

The next step merges the current functional DFDs with whatever additions and changes have been envisioned for the new system. The result is the set of new functional DFDs, which specify the business functions of the new system.

The set of new functional DFDs is the ideal system for the business under analysis. Free from the constraints of a still-all-too-limited technology, the new functional system reflects as accurately as possible the needs and wishes of business people as best they understand them and in their own terms.

It is also at this stage that design of an informational database begins. During structured analysis, analysts specify an informational database structure, which describes the informational content of files and their logical relationship to one another. This stage of the design does not consider any particular physical implementation of the database.

The informational database design is used by Process 3, which produces the design of a physical database to be managed by some database management program, such as IMS or ADABAS. I include Process 3 to make it clear that physical database design occurs sometime between structured analysis and structured design or during the design phase. In fact, database design tends to go through all the stages of the structured process. Typically, the physical database design is not fully consolidated until the implementation phase begins.

5.2.3 Define the new physical model

Once the best system to fulfill the needs of the users is specified, that system must be made to operate in a real-world environment. In this step of structured analysis, the analyst must prepare some alternative implementation plans for review by the user; these plans must cover projected costs and benefits, how much of the system will be automated, and whether the processing will be online or batch, disk or tape. These alternative plans must consider budget and timing constraints as well. The analyst and user then choose an implementation plan together.

5.2.4 Complete the structured specification

When the user and analyst have chosen the implementation plan that best fits the operating needs and management constraints, the analyst prepares a completed structured specification. It includes the new physical DFDs, the project dictionary, the structured English process descriptions, and the informational database design. With the structured specification in hand, design of program modules can begin (Process 4).

This rough outline of the steps of a structured analysis has been applied in many projects around the world. Its underlying principles are sound, its beneficial results are demonstrable. Yet, a structured project can get into trouble in many ways — for example, by lacking adequate interaction between user and analyst, by not maintaining the project dictionary, and by failing to excise unnecessary physical constraints. I will elaborate on some of these troubles in the following chapters. In particular, Chapter 7 goes into more detail about the structured analysis phase of a project.

5.3 Systems integration

Systems integration, Process 5, is often left out altogether; it involves determining the impact of the new system on the people and the organization of a business.

The fact that systems integration doesn't even appear in most life cycle diagrams suggests that an unfortunate historical trend continues to this day; that trend is systems developers' preference to focus on computer systems rather than on the people who must use the new system and who cannot be programmed as easily as a computer to perform new functions. From the outset of the project, developers must be aware of how the new system may change people's jobs. Performing systems integration fully requires the orientation, training, and perhaps transfer of people and functions.

An example of the effect of ignoring systems integration comes from the early history of business computing. Coming from a research environment, the early number crunching computers seemed most suitable for accounting applications. As a result, a company's data processing function was typically located in the treasurer's department or some similar financial area of the organization. Although the uses of computers became diversified, many companies retained the responsibility for data processing within the financial organization. As a result, professional data processors found themselves with such titles as senior financial analyst, long after it made any sense to consider financial applications part of their work. For many of even the largest corporations, it was not until the early 1970s that the data processing work was segregated and established in an independent information systems department.

Planning for systems integration begins at the same time as drawing the physical DFD of the existing business. Reviewing early physical DFDs, I often see dataflows that don't seem to make sense for a company's organization. These data anomalies come from functions that have changed faster than the bureaucratic structure to which they belong. As a result, people find themselves doing work that isn't relevant to their department or to their title. As people's jobs become part of the DFD, management must determine whether people are in the appropriate department and begin to explore the kind of training each person will need if his job changes as a result of the new system.

The planned systems integration becomes firm as the DFDs in a structured specification show functional groupings that make sense from the point of view of business data flow. The new functional DFDs strongly suggest a possible reorganization of part of the company along those functional lines. A system must fit into the business organization, or it will not live up to its potential, no matter how good it is.

Systems integration often erroneously includes a host of miscellaneous activities such as converting reports to new formats. Any file that needs to undergo such a change should be included in the scope of the project as part of the analysis/design/implementation sequence. I strongly urge including file conversions in the specification.

5.4 The partially structured project life cycle

Although the structured life cycle is designed to be used as a whole in developing a system, a project can make use of the structured life cycle methodology at any point. That is to say, if a traditional analysis has been completed for a project when the decision is made to use structured techniques, it may be more trouble than it's worth to back up and do a complete structured analysis from scratch. In this case, the structured designers must identify functional processes for the design phase and prepare thorough physical data flow diagrams which show these processes.

Let us look at an example: Managers at an insurance company call for a consultant when they feel traditional analysis is finished. The consultant insists that they back up and start from scratch, recommending a full training program in the structured analysis techniques. The managers are horrified, and the company rebels against the proposal. Instead, the company begins to draw structure charts without benefit of a structured specification.

This approach, while it requires considerable backtracking into analysis, is less time-consuming than if the company were to start again, and it yields a satisfactory system. The company's managers conclude at the successful end of the project that they wish they had started with structured analysis, but they are satisfied not to have restarted from scratch.

5.5 Beyond analysis

The other processes in the structured life cycle are beyond the scope of this book; they are treated in other texts, however. In particular, DeMarco discusses the details of hardware analysis (Process 8) as part of the overall life cycle,* and Yourdon and Constantine's *Structured Design* goes into detail on structured design, implementation, and testing.† In addition, Yourdon's *Managing the System Life Cycle* deals with the overall management and control of a software development project.‡

---

*DeMarco, op. cit.
†E. Yourdon and L. Constantine, *Structured Design: Fundamentals of a Discipline of Computer Program and Systems Design* (New York: Yourdon Press, 1978).
‡E. Yourdon, *Managing the System Life Cycle* (New York: Yourdon Press, 1982).

6

The Soft Factors

Structured analysis provides a clear method for developing a technical specification suitable for use by systems designers. However, the success of any project depends upon the relationships among the people who work on it and their ability to work as a team. I call these issues the soft factors because of the difficulty in measuring them and assigning values to them. This chapter considers what are good working relationships between users and analysts and what are successful project methods as the technical work begins in a structured project.

6.1 The user

Let's start our discussion with those who both begin and end the structured project: the users. Systems developers must always keep in mind that the user is instigator, guide, and eventual beneficiary of the structured project. It is the user for whom the analyst works ultimately, and failure to respond to this fact can only exacerbate the natural communication gap between technical and nontechnical people. The plan of structured analysis calls for frequent interaction between user and analyst so that the resulting structured system will blend the best of both business and technical considerations.

Frequent contributions by users are key to a successful structured project, and the burden of managing the delicate user-analyst interface rests on the analyst. To maximize the interaction between user and analyst, the analyst may need to propose the organization of the users' project team. The analyst needs to question the users skillfully to discover all necessary information about the business. He also must take the responsibility for coordinating interviews and reviews with users. He may need to arrange training for users who have no previous exposure to the structured methods.

But if the users' schedules will not permit a meeting, even the most conscientious analyst can accomplish nothing. Although the users generally realize that certain informational needs are not being met by current systems, these very inadequacies prevent them from staying close to the structured project. Running a business is demanding in the best of circumstances and can become even more so when done without adequate information support. It should come as no surprise then that user personnel are often reluctant to spend what seems like excessive time with the analysts, even though it is in the users' best interest to do so.

6.1.1 Who is the user?

To work with the user, the analyst must of course know who the user is. The user is the person or group of people who interact with the system in the course of running their business. They may be involved with the system daily or may be only tangentially aware of the system through the reports and analyses of data it produces. The users may be in any part of the company, and they may be technical or nontechnical.

Unfortunately, the user is often hard to identify. A major reason for this difficulty is that managers of user organizations typically have little or no idea of the user's role in the systems development process. This means that they know neither what work needs to be done by their groups nor what personnel to assign to do the work.

For the purposes of a structured analysis, categorizing users based on their relationship to the project development team is useful. Typically, the user is not just one person and often not even one organization. DeMarco finds three classes of user: the responsible user, the system owner, and the hands-on user.* Each of these classes may include a broad spectrum of people at different levels of the company.

The analyst's first priority is to identify the responsible users, who will review the project work, make suggestions for changes to it, and approve the structured specification. Typically, the responsible user is a project leader whose job is to coordinate day-to-day evolution of the

---

*T. DeMarco, *Structured Analysis and System Specification* (New York: Yourdon Press, 1979), p. 14.

system from the user's point of view and to recommend acceptance to a manager. The second type of user, the system owner, authorizes the expenditure of funds, but this person generally has little involvement with the project. Finally, there are the hands-on users, who typically know little or nothing about the project or about their eventual role in making the production system work day to day.

6.2 Organizing the project

The essential factor in organizing a structured project is establishing a healthy relationship between user and analyst. Through this rapport, the analyst can gain enough understanding of the scope of the user's business to be able to document it as a set of well-defined interacting processes that share well-defined data. This suggests that the analyst should interview people who both know the overall operation of the business and also can define data clearly.

6.2.1 The omnibus meeting

I suggest the following approach to starting off the structured project and establishing communication between user and analyst. I like to begin a structured project with a one- to two-day meeting (preferably a weekend retreat) of the entire project staff: users, analysts, managers, and anyone else connected with the project. I refer to this as the omnibus meeting, and define omnibus to mean "to, for, by, with, or from everybody," a good description of this meeting.

The purpose of this meeting is to encourage teamwork while developing a good first-cut physical DFD at the Figure 0 level (Section 6.2.2) and to establish walkthrough, review, and interview schedules (Section 6.2.3). However, from my point of view as a consultant and a therapist in psychological counseling, the most important goal is to involve the entire project team in an exercise in group dynamics — that is, to help the group members become aware of the way they interact and communicate with each other.

If, at this early point in the project, personal communication channels can develop among the team members, participants will probably be able to resolve conflicts when they occur in the project. I do not mean to publicize the omnibus meeting as an encounter group; yet because people do bring personal problems to the work environment, the meeting functions somewhat like an encounter group. People challenge each other's statements and actions as they work on the DFD and schedules and in this way learn to work together. If personal conflicts arise, they can be openly discussed. Developing schedules and a DFD are relatively safe topics and participants can work with these issues without feeling threatened. If nothing else, the omnibus session often shows what a dramatic lack of communication and understanding exists, even among people who have worked with each other for a long time. The meeting should be refereed by a disinterested outsider, preferably an experienced group leader, and preferably not an employee of the company.

The cost of this meeting in dollars and in time is more than offset by the benefits of a project that proceeds with a minimum of friction among the team members.

6.2.2 Teamwork

One purpose of the omnibus meeting is to explore what is becoming practice in the real world: team analysis. By recommending that the participants of this meeting work in teams, I mean to convey more than the assignment of several people to a project. The objective of this exercise is for *all* participants to develop a particular DFD during a team meeting, rather than have the work of one individual simply reviewed by the team. This approach particularly applies to developing the project's Figure 0 on the physical DFD. The omnibus meeting is a good forum to teach the techniques of team analysis.

My approach to teaching team analysis comes from the encounter group method, which requires the mediator not only to follow the technical agenda, but also to be constantly aware of the group's dynamics. During the first part of the meeting, I act as mediator and usually wield the chalk myself to show participants what I expect them to do at the board. Gradually, I encourage others to take the role of scribe and give at least half my attention to what's going on among the participants. A more detailed description of the drawing of Figure 0 is given in Chapter 7, Section 7.1.4.

The team approach has significant benefits and the method is gaining favor on structured projects. After implementing the team approach, projects report shorter development time, fewer omissions in the specification, and better communication among team members.

The team approach is not without its problems, however. One problem is finding objective reviewers who are not members of the team. Although a group of people working together can be effective in spotting errors and deficiencies, they can also reinforce each other's blind spots. For this reason, it is important to find people not involved with the work to participate in reviews.

Since both users and analysts are often involved in developing a particular DFD, it is difficult to find an objective reviewer who understands the system. One effective technique is to intentionally exclude one of the project members from a piece of the development. When the rest of the team has completed its work, the "outcast" is brought in to review the results. Another approach is to engage an experienced structured consultant who participates in reviews only.

Group reviews are an important part of working as a team. The next subsection discusses the team review of its members' work, called a *walkthrough*.

6.2.3 Walkthroughs

A walkthrough is a meeting whose purpose is to review a particular document, such as a DFD, for correctness and completeness. As stated before, an important goal of the omnibus meeting is to establish review schedules for reviews and walkthroughs early in the current systems documentation phase. The frequency of walkthroughs can vary somewhat from project to project, but if the time between meetings is more than two weeks, people tend to waste considerable time becoming reoriented to the subject under discussion. On the other hand, a frequency of less than a week doesn't give analysts much time to make significant advances; participants feel that they are doing nothing but having meetings.

Walkthroughs should be brief (thirty minutes long) and include only relevant people. Unless one is a consultant, there is nothing more boring and wasteful than sitting through a walkthrough of somebody else's department. Keeping meetings to the point and within the allotted time will help maintain attendance by everyone.

Scheduling weekly walkthrough sessions for one particular time (Tuesday or Wednesday morning is best) alerts all user personnel to keep that block of time available in case their part of the business is under scrutiny. Analysts should notify them well ahead of time if their presence is not needed.

Before the walkthrough, the analyst should prepare an agenda and overhead transparencies of the diagrams to be reviewed. Hard copy of all diagrams and structured English should be distributed the day before the meeting. During the meeting, it is helpful to walk through each diagram, one piece of data at a time. Overlays for each piece of data, showing in color the path followed by each input until it becomes output, help participants to follow the discussion. Since the benefit of a walkthrough is the feedback from the attendees, leave plenty of space on the diagrams and next to the structured English for suggestions and corrections.

In *Structured Walkthroughs,* Ed Yourdon outlines the many types of walkthrough and presents the people and rules relevant to each one.* I suggest reading that book for more information.

---

*E. Yourdon, *Structured Walkthroughs,* 2nd ed. (New York: Yourdon Press, 1978).

Walkthroughs are nonjudgmental in nature. Errors in DFDs are usually the result of misunderstanding between a user and an analyst, and to lay the blame on the analyst misses this point. The main idea of the user walkthrough is to identify these misunderstandings as early as possible and correct them. In user interviews, the analyst has recorded (in DFD form) what he thought the user had said; during the walkthrough, the user verifies that the analyst has not misinterpreted him. In this respect, user walkthroughs differ from design or program walkthroughs, in which errors often are due to faulty logic by the designer or programmer.

Observe that the term *walkthrough* is a catchall that encompasses almost any kind of review, including the analyst's desk-check of DFDs before they are presented. Some of the characteristics that distinguish walkthroughs from each other are their degree of formality (from formal to informal), the type of product to be walked through (specification, design, code, functional or physical DFD), and the attendees (user, manager, analyst, designer, or programmer).

The main purpose of any walkthrough is to review a piece of work for correctness and completeness. All in all, the many rules and approaches to walkthroughs boil down to common sense; use the walkthrough to register suggestions for change rather than make ad hoc changes on the spot. Presumably, the analyst had good reasons for writing the DFD as it is presented, but the stress of a presentation may dull memory of these reasons. A change based on someone's immediate reaction that the diagram is wrong is likely to be premature.

6.2.4 A project scheduling method

As an aid in scheduling systems development projects, managers typically use a commercial methodology, which provides guidelines for planning the stages of the project. Many such methodologies do not state the techniques to be used for the technical specification, so structured analysis fits with them as well as any other technique does. DFDs themselves can also help with the scheduling of a project. To my knowledge, very few people other than my clients and I have used the DFD technique as a management tool in its own right, even though DFDs are an ideal way to assist in resource allocation, estimating, and status reporting.

A DFD works very much like any other critical path diagram, except in a DFD events are actually driven by critical data paths — and what could be more fitting for a methodology that so highly touts the idea of systems being data-driven? When a DFD is used for scheduling, I call it a management DFD.

The management data flow diagram can be used during analysis to indicate when certain DFDs are scheduled to be done, or during design and implementation to show the completion dates for the products of those phases. Because of continuous updating, the analysis DFDs are as accurate during implementation as during analysis and design, and so they can continue to be used for scheduling later project phases. If they are not still accurate, then the project is in trouble because someone is making unreported changes.

Because DFDs are changing constantly during analysis, the scheduling will have to be revised in step with the technical changes. Nonetheless, the technical documents themselves provide an excellent medium for keeping track of scheduling changes. Let's look first at the new DFD notation, and then at its use.

To implement the management data flow diagram, I have extended the notation to allow several dates, a resource name, a medium and time for transferring data between processes, and a time estimated for a process, as shown in Figure 6.1. The manager does not necessarily draw an entire set of DFDs for scheduling, but uses the high-level DFDs as they evolve, and simply adds dates and resources.

The need for any of the additional notation varies considerably from project to project and from phase to phase within a project. The notational scheme contains options for specifying things; it does not require the use of all its facilities.

Each dataflow can carry up to four dates, although typically not all of them appear. The meaning of these dates varies depending upon the stage of the structured project being scheduled. For example, during analysis, the dates can refer to points when a set of lower-level DFDs are complete enough to guarantee their accuracy. During production, after a completed system is installed, the dates indicate times when data are actually produced by the process. The four dates shown in Figure 6.1 are the earliest and latest dates available, earliest date usable, and latest deadline, as explained below:

- *earliest date available:* This date appears just above a dataflow where it leaves a process; it indicates the earliest time at which the dataflow is reasonably likely to leave the process that produces it. If we are scheduling analysis activities using a Layer 1 diagram, this is the earliest date that the analyst is likely to have finished all lower-level DFDs of a particular Layer 1 process.

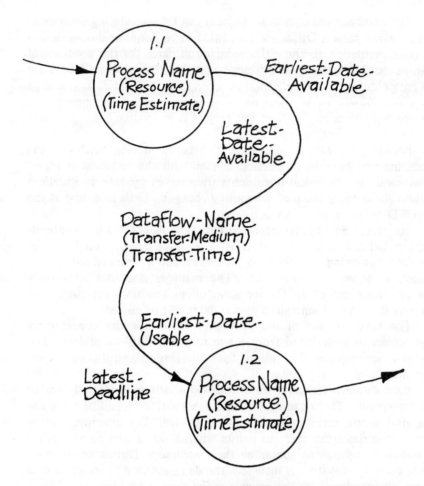

Figure 6.1. Management DFD for scheduling.

- *latest date available:* This date appears just below a dataflow as it leaves a process; it can be either the guaranteed latest date that a dataflow is ready for use by another process or the latest date we can afford to have it available if we are to finish something on time. During analysis, a dataflow that is ready for use is one whose contents are correct. In other words, the analyst who completes the diagramming for a process guarantees that the dataflow is as shown on the DFD and as defined in the project dictionary.

- *earliest date usable:* This date appears just above a dataflow where it enters a process; it indicates the earliest date on which a dataflow is likely to be available to the process that needs it.

- *latest deadline:* This date appears just below a dataflow as it enters a process; this is the final date by which a dataflow must have arrived at a process if the schedule is to be preserved.

There is a reason for having possibly different dates at each end of the dataflow. In a real-world system, data may not flow automatically and instantly from one process to another. Frequently, data must be carried by some medium to a process, and this takes time. The medium and transfer time notations appear in parentheses below the dataflow name.

The Number One Beverage Mart operational system, described in Chapter 3, shows the effect of transfer time and transfer medium. Dates or times inserted into Figure 3.14 would represent actual data processing in the real world. The Payment-Auth dataflow is shown going from the Check Shipment process to the Pay For Shipment process, although no medium is shown for this movement. If the system were to rely on company mail to do this data transfer, a significant amount of real time could elapse before the Payment-Auth is actually usable by the process that needs it. The medium and transfer time notations are convenient ways of indicating these real-world delays.

Two additional items may be noted within a process on the management DFD. One is the name of the resource or resources doing the process. Depending again on the project phase being diagrammed, the resource might be the person carrying out the process or an analyst charged with layering this piece of the system. The amount of time (in any convenient units) allocated to do the work required can also be noted.

Figures 6.2 and 6.3 show Figure 0 and Figure 1, respectively, of a set of DFDs that describe the preparation for presenting a particular course. The two diagrams are a good example of the scheduling of a production system. The dates in Figure 6.2 reflect the deadline to present a course called Introduction to Structured Projects (ISP) on September 25 and 26. These same diagrams were used in scheduling the analysis with different dates and resources. As I mentioned previously, a management DFD does not need to show all dates and other items. If dates are used on more than one level, then they must balance in the same way that dataflow names must balance between levels.

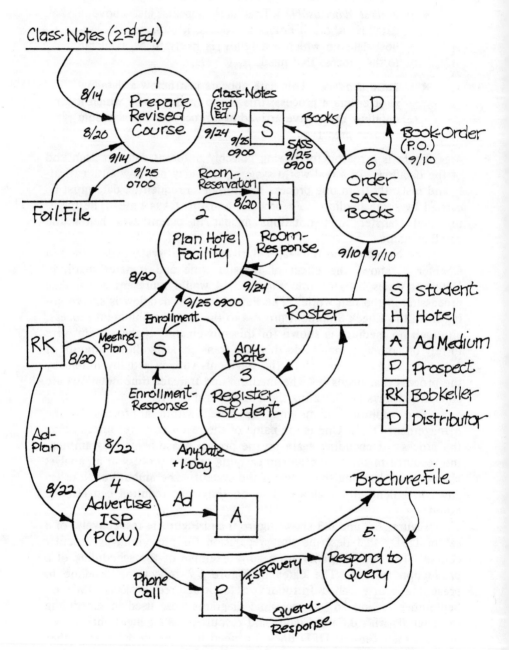

Figure 6.2. Figure 0 of course presentation example.

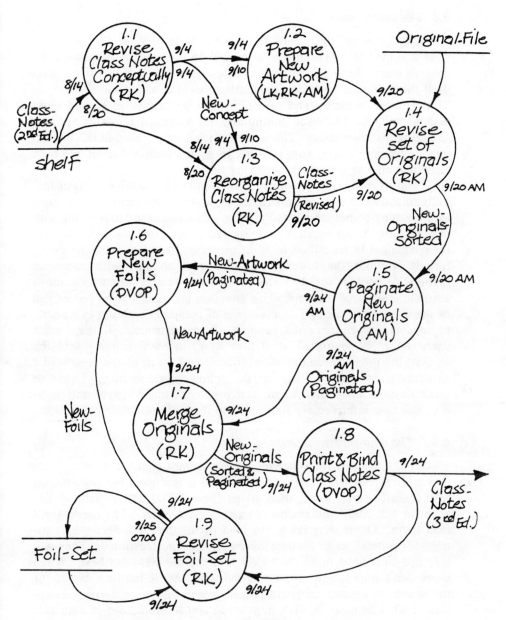

Figure 6.3. Figure 1 of course presentation example.

6.3 The absent user

In discussing the omnibus meeting, teamwork, and reviews, we have assumed that appropriate users will be available to work with the analysis team. But what if they're not available? What does the analyst do if the user won't interact frequently or even at all?

There is a clear trend in data processing to give more and more responsibility to the user community for organizing, accessing, and analyzing its own data. The commercial success of natural English query systems strongly suggests that many nontechnical users are both eager and able to take on this responsibility.

Unfortunately, many others show a crippling unwillingness or inability to approach data processing except in the most remote ways, such as by reading computer-printed reports. This resistance to working with the computer arises because business people are often too busy running their business to take time to learn new ways, because company policy forbids any but the lowest-level employees to deal with computer matters, or because the data processing group is unwilling to relinquish absolute control of the data. This situation prevents a large percentage of the users from taking full advantage of computer technology's ability to support and enhance the running of their business. If responsible users cannot be identified, or if they won't interact regularly with the analyst, the project becomes more difficult and much of the benefit of a structured approach is lost. In the following subsections, I present three ways to solve the absent user problem: the do-it-yourself solution, the user intermediary solution, and the end user training solution.

6.3.1 The do-it-yourself solution

If the analyst, for whatever reason, cannot conduct regular meetings and reviews with user personnel, and if the users are not familiar with the structured tools, then giving them DFDs and structured English for self-study and review is guaranteed disaster. The users won't read them. Or, if they do try to read them, they will become so enmeshed in detail as to become overwhelmed and frustrated. They will give up, convinced more than ever that the old ways are best. When users don't understand structured specifications, it is much better for the analyst to use the DFDs to prepare a step-by-step narrative description of what happens to each transaction and to each piece of data as it is processed by the proposed system.*

---

*These narratives can be organized and layered in the same way the DFDs are layered. Preparing these narratives is an unfortunate and unnecessary burden on the analyst and should be avoided if at all possible. Nonetheless, these narratives can close a breach in communication with users. They give users much of the benefit of a structured approach while allowing them to digest it in a form with which they are already comfortable.

6.3.2 The user intermediary solution

One solution to the too-busy-to-bother user is being explored by an increasing number of companies. The solution is to assign a user intermediary to the project. Frequently, such people come from the operations side of the business — from marketing or manufacturing, for example. These user intermediaries bring to the project a firsthand awareness of the user's point of view, and should have more than a passing acquaintance with data processing, although they are seldom data processing professionals.

The user intermediary is the analyst's primary source of information about the business and about how to transform that information into a systems specification. Where there are gaps in the intermediary's knowledge of the business, the intermediary consults the user for clarification. In some cases, such contact with the users may spark their interest and actually convince them to participate somewhat in the project.

Unfortunately, the user intermediary does not provide a complete solution to the problem of user-analyst interaction. Producing a finished structured specification requires a detailed understanding of all parts of the business under analysis, and one person does not usually possess such comprehensive understanding. A structured project requires involved users if it is to be as successful as possible.

6.3.3 The training solution

One of the joys of my experience has been teaching structured analysis to end users and managers, people who typically know little about data processing. Often, these people have been so battered by traditional approaches to systems development that they come with minds open to anything new that may give them a system that does what they want it to do.

The best time for this training is just before the omnibus meeting. The timing is important since members of the user community often feel somehow inferior to the systems people, who presumably are brimming with esoteric knowledge about computers. Exposing the users to some of that esoteric knowledge helps them feel more on an equal footing with the technical staff at the omnibus meeting.

User training also makes the analysis phase go more smoothly since the user can now be an active partner in the development of DFDs. More than once I have attended user interviews at which a user, frustrated at trying to explain to an analyst what his business does, has picked up the chalk and started drawing a DFD to clarify what he was saying.

Not everyone in the user organization needs to be trained to draw DFDs, and no one in that organization needs to have the in-depth understanding that an analyst does. However, certainly anyone who will attend walkthroughs or who will be interviewed by an analyst can benefit from at least one or two days of training in structured analysis techniques. This training includes lecture and workshop exposure to the same material that is presented to analysts: DFDs, structured English, the data dictionary, and so forth. Note that you can't train users in the same way you train systems people: Most of the jargon regarding file structures and operating systems would only cloud the essentially business-oriented nature of the analytical process. The emphasis for users is more on reviewing and evaluating a proposed system than on specifying it.

Since many nontechnical people feel threatened by having to learn about computers, I usually begin a course in structured analysis for users by reassuring them: I tell the class that the course has practically nothing to do with computers, that the analysis phase is a business-oriented task, and that the hardest thing I'll ask them to do is to look in detail at their day-to-day work.

Looking at the details of their work is a hard task since most people carry out their daily responsibilities with virtually no awareness of what they're doing or how they do it. This is a necessity and actuality of living in the world. We tend to make all those tasks with which we are comfortable into unconscious reflex actions, saving our conscious awareness for the unfamiliar, the constantly arising crises. If we needed to analyze every minor task, such as dialing the telephone, little work of consequence would ever get done.

If for some reason the users have not yet been trained, I often take some time at the first interview or at the omnibus meeting to explain the structured process, particularly DFDs. I orient the users to the techniques by walking through a DFD representation of my own recipe for omelette complète, accompanied by a project dictionary and a process description. The purpose is to show that the structured tools are as applicable to non-data-processing tasks as they are to the highly sophisticated systems the project will build.

I show users the context diagram in Figure 6.4 and point out that it lists everything needed to prepare this dish. Not only that, but the names for ingredients are what the users would expect to call them. The names in any system should give the reader a good idea of what the components are. If the reader needs to know something in more detail, he can turn to the project dictionary for an explicit definition.

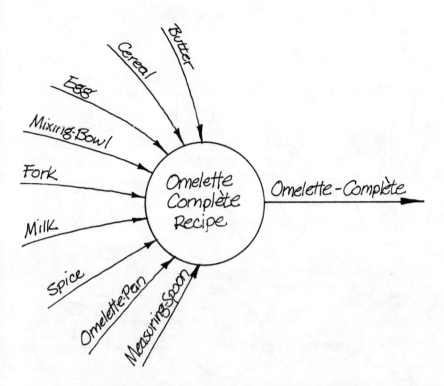

Figure 6.4. Context diagram for omelette complète.

At this point, I flip to the project dictionary and read through one of the definitions with the users: spice, for example. As shown in this recipe's project dictionary, which follows Figure 6.5, spice can mean either salt, curry, or thyme, and the dictionary also tells what measures to use for each.

There is only one DFD for this system, shown in Figure 6.5, but it includes most of the salient features of any DFD. As I walk through the diagram, I describe the dataflows, sources and sinks, and processes, although I don't usually use the DFD terminology at this point. In this activity, I do try to point out the simultaneity of processes. For example, there's no reason why the milk can't be warming (Process 3) while the cook breaks the egg (Process 1). I also point out that a process is driven by the data it needs to do its job and usually can't run until the data are available. For example, the cook can't add milk (Process 4) until both warm milk and the spiced mixture are available. I also indicate that the data objects (mixing bowl, for instance) are named on the DFD and that they each are described in the project dictionary.

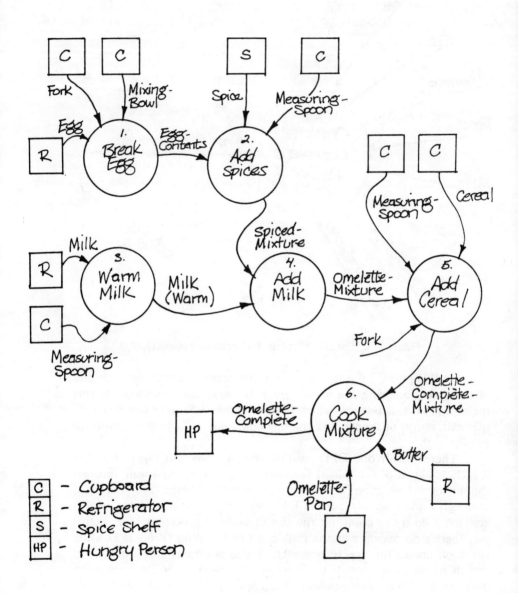

Figure 6.5. Figure 0 of the omelette complète example.

Omelette Complète Recipe
Project Dictionary

Butter   = *To lubricate Omelette-Pan, 2 tbsp*
Cereal   = *Walnut Acres 12-Grain Cereal, 1 heaping tbsp*
Egg   = *Large size*

Egg-Contents   = *Broken Egg*
                   = Mixing-Bowl + $\frac{2}{2}${Yolk} + $\frac{2}{2}${White}

Milk   = *To tenderize omelette, 2 tbsp*

Omelette-Mixture   = *Omelette before Cereal is added*
                   = Spiced-Mixture + Milk (Warm)

Omelette-Complète-Mixture=   *Delicious, robust breakfast*
                         =   Omelette-Mixture + Cereal

Spiced-Mixture   = *Eggs and Spices*
                  = Egg-Contents + ^{3}{Spice}

Spice   = *Flavoring for Omelette*
        = $\begin{bmatrix} \text{Salt} & \text{*1/8 tsp*} \\ \text{Curry} & \text{*3 shakes*} \\ \text{Thyme} & \text{*1/8 tsp crushed*} \end{bmatrix}$

Omelette Complète Recipe Process Description

Process 1: Break Egg
1.   Get a small Mixing-Bowl.
2.   Do the following twice:
      2.1   Get an Egg.
      2.2   Break it into the Mixing-Bowl.

Process 2: Add Spice
1.   For each Spice desired:
      1.1   Add it to the Egg-Contents.

Process 3: Warm Milk
1.   Warm 2 tbsp of Milk to room temperature.

Process 4: Add Milk
1.   Add 2 tbsp of warm Milk to the Spiced-Mixture.

Process 5: Add Cereal
1.   Add 1 heaping tbsp of Cereal to the Omelette-Mixture.
2.   Whip the Omelette-Mixture lightly to wet the dry ingredients.

3. Allow to stand at least five minutes while the wet and dry ingredients combine.

Process 6: Cook Mixture

1. Warm the Omelette-Pan to a medium heat.

2. Melt 1 tbsp of Butter in the Omelette-Pan.

3. Pour the Omelette-Complète-Mixture into the Omelette-Pan, and whip it until it is warmed evenly.

4. As the mixture cooks, move the uncooked part under the cooked part until a desirable consistency is achieved throughout.

5. Fold the cooked Omelette-Complète-Mixture in thirds, and melt the remaining 1 tbsp of Butter in the Omelette-Pan.

6. Serve the Omelette-Complète on a warm plate. Voilà!

To conclude the discussion, I take all of the individual process descriptions and string them together into a single structured English narrative. This looks much more like a recipe than users would expect to see. Doing this helps to point out the arbitrariness of process boundaries. With a system as simple as this recipe, it might well make more sense to use a single process description instead of a DFD.

Omelette Complète Recipe Process Description

1. Get a small Mixing-Bowl.

2. Do the following twice:

    2.1 Get an Egg.

    2.2 Break it into the Mixing-Bowl.

3. For each Spice desired:

    3.1 Add it to the Egg-Contents.

4. Warm 2 tbsp of Milk to room temperature.

5. Add 2 tbsp of warm Milk to the Spiced-Mixture.

6. Add 1 heaping tbsp of Cereal to the Omelette-Mixture.

7. Whip the Omelette-Mixture lightly to wet the dry ingredients.

8. Allow to stand at least five minutes while the wet and dry ingredients combine.

9. Warm the Omelette-Pan to a medium heat.

10. Melt 1 tbsp of Butter in the Omelette-Pan.

11. Pour the Omelette-Complète-Mixture into the Omelette-Pan, and whip it until it is warmed evenly.

12. As the mixture cooks, move the uncooked part under the cooked part until a desirable consistency is achieved throughout.

13. Fold the cooked Omelette-Complète-Mixture in thirds, and melt the remaining 1 tbsp of Butter in the Omelette-Pan.

14. Serve the Omelette-Complète on a warm plate. Voilà!

6.4 Conclusion

In this chapter, I have discussed the soft factors, which play a role in the success of a project equal to that of the more technical methods of structured analysis.

It is all too easy to downplay the soft factors since they deal with the fuzzy areas of morale, attitude, and human relationships. It seems impossible to me to quantify these areas, but this is no reason to ignore them. On the contrary, the very irrationality of human behavior should force project leadership to consider people issues carefully. Only by being constantly aware of what goes on behind the scenes can management avoid being tripped up by the soft factors.

All of the components — the tools, the methods, and the people — are now in place for an in-depth look at analysis as a process. In the next chapter, we proceed through the steps of a structured analysis, seeing how to apply all of the information provided to achieve a smoothly functioning structured project.

7

The Process of Analysis

Analysis is more than simply the combination of its hard and soft factors. The tools, or hard factors, of structured analysis provide an excellent medium to specify the technical aspects of a system, but their successful application requires an understanding of the process of analysis. Similarly, identifying the effects of the soft factors (project organization and the relationships among team members) is useless without an understanding of the tasks that the team carries out.

Analysis consists of several steps that are more or less distinct in theory. In practice, completing one step before going to another is seldom possible or even necessary. The effect is that various pieces of the system may be in different stages of analysis simultaneously.

Furthermore, a stage may be repeated to some extent later in the project. For example, analysis may be performed on the system at a high level; that is, analysts may draw only the first one or two layers of a DFD before going on to the next stages, whose DFDs are also limited to one or two levels. The analysts return later to carry out the earlier stages in more detail. This process is called iteration.

Allowing steps on a project to iterate goes counter to the majority of management styles; management typically insists on a carefully phased approach, with definite deliverables at the end of each phase. Structured analysis doesn't prevent you from having deliverables. However, I prefer to call them reviewables, since this supports the structured analysis notion that its tools are working documents, always subject to change.

This chapter and the next look at structured analysis as a process; they explain the steps and give them some sequence, while emphasizing that each step is iterative by nature. The six steps in a structured analysis are these:

- making a first-cut physical DFD of the entire current system
- functionalizing the current DFDs
- developing mini-models of the new system
- completing the new functional DFDs
- creating the new physical DFDs
- completing the structured specification

Each step is discussed in sequence.

7.1 Making a first-cut DFD of the current system

The analysis phase begins as analysts document the current system. If computer systems are in place, they are included in the systems description. If the present environment is totally manual, the processes in the current system are the people or the functions that the people perform.

People often believe that since the current system is being replaced, documenting it is irrelevant. However, even though the implementation of business functions may be changing, most of the functions being performed will be carried over to the new system. Failure to document what the current system does frequently leads to extensive revisions of the new system when it goes into a production environment. Taking shortcuts on the documentation of the current system is seldom, if ever, cost-effective.

Developing a first-cut DFD of the current system requires completing several major tasks:

- assembling the entire project team for the omnibus meeting (see Chapter 6)
- starting a project dictionary
- developing a context diagram, which delineates the scope of the project in terms of the inputs and outputs
- evolving the overview of the system's processes, Figure 0
- establishing review schedules

These five tasks are treated in the subsections below.

7.1.1 The omnibus meeting

The first major task is to assemble the entire project team for the omnibus meeting, as described in Chapter 6. All of the other tasks can be at least initiated at this meeting, as discussed below.

7.1.2 The project dictionary

Before any other work begins, the first task for the omnibus meeting is to address the project dictionary. As discussed in Chapter 2, the project dictionary contains the most complete and current information about the project, including a description of all data and processes as far as they are known. Starting the dictionary means assigning a project librarian and deciding on which of the methods described in Chapter 2 are to be used for maintaining the dictionary.

7.1.3 The context diagram

According to structured analysis theory, the first diagram in the set of current DFDs is the context diagram. It contains a single process bubble that is named for the entire project: "payroll system," for example. The context diagram defines the scope of the structured project by showing what physical data the system takes in and puts out. In this way, it shows unambiguously the boundaries of the structured project. In fact, in most projects, developers start out not knowing where the boundaries are. Developers may know they must develop a new payroll system or inventory system, but they may not know exactly how much of the existing system will be replaced. For example, they may be confused as to whether rewriting the payroll system includes rewriting the tax system, which feeds payroll.

Generally, not until well into the specification of the current physical system does an accurate context diagram emerge. Nevertheless, a first-cut context diagram is valuable in beginning work on the overview of the system's processes. Enough information is usually available to enable developers to complete a rough draft at the omnibus meeting. Some documentation of the current system probably exists already, although it is usually incomplete and inaccurate. The feasibility study also may contain an attempt to define the new project. This documentation should be used as a basis to rough out the context diagram of the project.

7.1.4 The overview: Figure 0

Once a version of the context diagram has been drawn, the next step is to develop the overview of the system's processes. Called Figure 0, this diagram is the highest-level DFD. The goal of this activity is to show all major parts of the system on a single page, while minimizing the complexity of the diagram.

The method for evolving Figure 0 is simple to describe, although in practice it can be lengthy and stressful. It is the same procedure given in Chapter 3. The omnibus meeting is a good place to start this diagram, since the experts on most of the relevant parts of the business should be assembled there.

To evolve Figure 0, start with one input on the context diagram, however rough that diagram may be, and document the processing of that input until it becomes one of the outputs on the context diagram. The group at the omnibus meeting may fail to do this because the context diagram is incomplete; in that case, one or more new outputs may be added to it. The group may also fail to completely describe the processing of an input because its processing is not well known. If so, the processing can be left as is, awaiting further investigation.

Next, repeat the procedure until all inputs have been dealt with to some degree. If not all the outputs have been generated during this procedure, take one of them and work backward, documenting the generation of that output. The group will probably discover more inputs to the context diagram. Perhaps some of the input processing that was left hanging will be discovered to connect to these outputs in ways not known earlier.

When the group has finished, it should have a (usually very) rough first-cut of Figure 0. It is unlikely that the group can complete a Figure 0 at the omnibus meeting, but it can usually discover most of the informational content. The lead analyst can take care of polishing the figure, working alone and consulting with various users if necessary. However, the more polishing done by the whole group during the omnibus meeting the better.

People in a brainstorming session, such as the omnibus meeting, do not think at a uniform level of detail. As a result, the evolved Figure 0 is probably very large and includes too much detail in some areas and not enough in others. The analyst's job in polishing is to repartition the group's Figure 0 so that the system is depicted by a reasonable number of processes of roughly consistent complexity. Everyone should agree that these processes accurately represent the project.

How many processes to allow on a single diagram frequently becomes an unnecessarily time-consuming issue. The theory of structured analysis urges an upper limit of nine processes on a single-page

DFD; this limit, while not completely arbitrary, can vary depending on the system under analysis. Nonetheless, nine processes and their associated dataflows constitute a considerable amount of information to put on one page, and so it may be a good working limit.

In developing a Figure 0 DFD for a complex project, an analyst will probably derive twenty or more processes that must be shown. In such a case, it is usually possible to group these twenty (or more) processes into two or more subsystems. Figure 0 then shows the subsystems, numbered with integers from 1 to N, and the original twenty or more processes are shown on the next layer of DFDs as the detail of Figures 1 to N; this is a completely acceptable approach. Information from overly detailed areas should be saved, since it can be used to refine Figure 0 processes as analysis proceeds.

7.1.5 Review schedules

User review schedules are also best established at the omnibus meeting, when everyone can discuss them together. As suggested in Chapter 6, meeting for reviews every week or two is good, although the schedule will probably change as the project proceeds. In addition to user reviews, regular analyst reviews are necessary if there is more than one analyst assigned to the project. Since Figure 0 shows the entire system as being composed of processes that are independent of one another except for the data they share, each Figure 0 process could be assigned to a different analyst for independent work. Regular analyst reviews are needed to guarantee that if any Figure 0 dataflows change as a result of deeper analysis, the change is reviewed with the analyst responsible for the process at the other end of the dataflow.

Reviews are held not only to ensure technical accuracy, but also to motivate team members after the omnibus meeting. The omnibus meeting generates excitement about the project, and on-going reviews use that momentum to keep users involved during the entire project.

With these early tasks completed, the detailed work of producing a structured specification can begin.

7.2 Functionalizing the current physical DFD

The first-cut physical DFD documents the current system by showing physical entities, such as Sales Department. The analysts may then draw several layers of DFDs, showing Sales Department broken into entities like Advertising Department and Order Processing Department. In fact, the business can be completely described with mainly physical processes, files, and data. This is the current physical description or DFD of the system.

However, the goal in documenting the current system is to arrive at a functional description of it, a description that omits people and physical processes as much as possible. Eventually, every physical DFD has to be turned into its functional equivalent.

The analyst can do this physical-to-functional transformation either in strict sequence (first physical DFDs, then functional ones), or he can do it more or less continually as the current systems documentation proceeds. The second approach, my preference, means that as the analyst is about to write down a physical process, he automatically starts to functionalize it, unless he doesn't know yet what functions it performs.

Hardly any DFDs at this stage are completely physical or functional, and so whether they are called physical or functional really amounts to whether physical or functional processes and data preponderate on them. I don't make as sharp a distinction between the current physical and current logical diagrams as does the theory of structured analysis, since they tend to blend together naturally. When you start to think about physical processes, they tend to turn into the functional processes that describe what people are doing. For example, consider a Figure 0 DFD that shows a living, physical process, Mary, with certain data inputs and outputs. The work of structured analysis is to break a high-level process, such as Mary, into smaller pieces so that one can understand the elementary functions Mary performs. To do this — to go below Figure 0 — the analyst must ask the question, What does Mary do? As soon as the analyst begins to answer that question, he is changing Mary from a physical to a functional process.

My approach to developing the current system DFDs is to functionalize only to the degree the user feels comfortable with. If this means documenting the whole system with physical data and processes, then that's a good start. However, as analysis moves along, I encourage replacement of the physical items with their functional equivalents as early as possible.

Developing current DFDs is the part of structured analysis that most heavily involves interviews with users, mainly because they're the only ones who know their business. While the analyst is writing down the current system on paper, the users are telling him how they would like things to be in the new system.

Hence, the analyst's job is both to document the current system and to note (in DFD form whenever possible) the changes the users want. Going back for a second round of individual interviews is a significant burden on a user, particularly if he feels he told the analyst all of the desired changes at the first interview. A second interview to discuss changes to the system will not turn up nearly as many good new ideas as will the interview to discuss the current system.

A popular pitfall in documenting the current system is to document too much, and so to extend this phase much longer than necessary. Remember that the goal of documenting the current environment is to arrive at a statement (DFD) of only those data and processes that will be affected by the new system. For example, if only the tax system is going to change, there is little point in diagramming the entire payroll system. On the other hand, the analyst must document enough of the existing system to be sure all affected functions of the business are included.

One further suggestion in developing the current physical and functional diagrams is to always be ready to scrap what has been done and to start again. In my classes, the teams with the best results are those that get something on paper quickly instead of just talking about it. In the real world, the temptation to wait until you have the perfect system in mind before writing anything is almost too much for some people. I recommend that work begin on a chalkboard so that false starts are easily corrected without having to rewrite the parts that are correct.

7.3 Developing mini-models of the new system

The analyst must put down on paper new ideas for system changes as they emerge, however simple or complex they may be. These new ideas come not only from the individual user interviews; they also may have been proposed during the survey or at walkthrough sessions. During a walkthrough or a user interview, the analyst often has difficulty keeping track of ideas for system changes since he is focusing on the current system. Assigning someone to write down the new ideas for subsequent analysis may be worthwhile.

The mini-model is perhaps the most useful way of capturing ideas to go into the new system. A mini-model is a complete specification of a piece of the system: It includes a DFD to describe the data processing; dictionary notation for the data inputs and outputs; and structured English to describe the processes.

The simple example of Figure 7.1 shows my technique for preparing a mini-model. Here, as everywhere throughout the analysis documentation, complete definitions of dictionary entries are not necessary at the outset; however, dictionary entries for every dataflow and file are necessary.

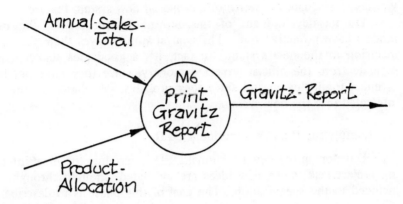

Data Definitions

Product-Allocation = *Percentage of sales attributable to each product*

Annual-Sales-Total = *Total net sales for the previous year*

Gravitz-Report = *Showing amount of sales for the previous year attributable to each product*

Product-Name =

Product-$ = *Amount of sales for the previous year attributable to each product*

Product-% = *Temporary storage for Product-Allocation*

Description for Process M6

> For each Product on the Product-Allocation
>> Set Product-% = Product-Allocation
>> Set Product-$ = Annual-Sales-Total × Product-%
>> Display Product-Name, Product-%, Product-$
> Display Annual-Sales-Total

Figure 7.1. Mini-model for the Print Gravitz Report process.

A mini-model does not have to be as simple as that shown in Figure 7.1; they often are considerably more complex. There is no reason that a mini-model can't have layered DFDs and multiple process descriptions as would any other specification.

Being able to examine a complete structured specification for a piece of the new system helps the user who proposed the change to be clearer about the details of a perceived need. It also helps project reviewers to evaluate the worth of a proposed new system feature.

During development of the current system DFDs, the mini-models have no active role. The analyst simply saves them for future inclusion in the new system. In fact, it's a good idea to keep them separate from the official project dictionary, since they have not been accepted for inclusion and since they probably will change as they are integrated into the new system.

7.4 Completing the new functional DFD

Developing the new functional DFD is certainly the most interesting project task, since new ideas are evaluated, thought through, and included in the specification. The goal of this phase is to describe the ideal system for a particular business environment; "ideal" means the system that most closely fits the needs of the business in order to run at its best. Whereas the current system DFD represents a system limited both by the history of technology and by the business environment as it has been, the new functional system is relatively unrestrained by technological limitations and other real-world constraints.

This stage begins as soon as someone has an idea about how the system should change. If the analyst has had the foresight to accumulate mini-models during the description of the current system, then much of the work to build the new functional DFD is already finished. The analyst's task now is to merge these mini-models into the current DFD, deleting or replacing old processes when necessary and adding the new.

Integrating the new mini-models into the current system is one of the main tasks of the new logical phase. This may be as simple as adding the new pieces, or it may require replacing a substantial number of existing processes. Generally, the analyst can work with the individual DFDs to add, change, and delete as required.

DeMarco suggests an alternative method:* Construct a paste-up of all bottom-level diagrams and connect the dataflows across DFD boundaries; this represents the entire current system in a single diagram. The analyst now marks all the processes that must change and, conceptually, removes them from the diagram. The void (Domain of Change) left by removing those processes is filled with the new system replacements.

---

*T. DeMarco, *Structured Analysis and System Specification* (New York: Yourdon Press, 1979), pp. 258ff.

The expanded DFD can take the better part of a day to construct and may yield little information that is not intuitively obvious. This method does have the significant benefit of forcing rigorous balancing of all DFDs and may be worthwhile if there is some question about the validity of balancing done previously.

The second major task of this step is to replace existing physical files with a set of normalized logical files that minimally satisfy the accesses peculiar to this project. (This subject is treated in Chapter 8). Frequently, the analyst can derive a set of logical files intuitively with considerably less effort than a formal derivation of those files would require. However, if the analyst finds the project members thrashing about, trying first one set of files then another, a rigorous derivation may be well worth the effort. DeMarco and Gane and Sarson both have excellent descriptions of the derivation technique.* Of course, if the project is constrained to keep an existing file intact, there is nothing to do but carry it over to the new diagrams.

When the logical file diagrams are complete, they are turned over to a database designer for implementation in a physical file system. As always, the project dictionary must be updated to describe the new system dataflows and files accurately.

A seldom fully exploited benefit of the new functional work is that analysts and users can look objectively at the way a business should be run, describe that way in the new functional DFDs, and then use the new system to guide reorganization of the business. Unfortunately, it is much more typical to allow technological and organizational limitations to dictate the allowable changes.

These limitations insert themselves automatically and forcefully as you try to physicalize the new functional system later. I strongly suggest that you use the new functional DFD to find the ideal accounting system or personnel system, and leave reality to the next stage of analysis.

7.5 Creating the new physical DFD

The new logical DFDs should describe something close to the ideal system for your business, since structured analysis has encouraged you to be free from real-world constraints. With the task of creating new physical DFDs, the real world of politics and current technology returns, often with a vengeance.

---

*Ibid., pp. 233-56; and C. Gane and T. Sarson, *Structured Systems Analysis: Tools & Techniques* (New York: Improved System Technologies, 1977), pp. 169-202.

The new physical stage of a structured project is intended to constrain your ideal system to particular physical situations and devices. Among the issues to be dealt with in this phase are the use of automated versus manual implementation of processes, centralized versus distributed processes, online versus batch access, and various input/output media.

Frequently, most of these decisions have been made far in advance, including the choice of the physical devices for operating the system and the time allotted for implementation. If there are still unresolved issues, the analyst has to figure out the costs and benefits of alternative implementations, and to review them with the users. In any case, the new logical DFDs must be modified to fit the new physical constraints.

Producing the new physical DFDs should be a fairly simple task. All the analyst is doing is adding processes and dataflows to specify the interfaces between logical data in the new logical DFDs and their physical forms in the real world. An output dataflow called Pay-Data, for example, may need a process that converts the logical Pay-Data to the physical paycheck format it will have in the real world.

Unfortunately, in most cases, producing the new physical DFDs is not so simple. There are two main reasons why this often becomes a difficult task:

- The new logical DFDs are incomplete.

- Developers and users cannot decide on implementation hardware and procedures.

If you find yourself wanting to add to the new logical diagrams more than relatively simple data transportation processes, the work of the new logical phase was probably inadequate. The analysts have not finished the new logical diagrams unless they have made all major decisions regarding functional business processing and the content of all input and output dataflows. For example, showing a final output called Pay-Data is not acceptable when some of the computations for deductions have not yet been done.

The second problem, implementation decisions, is often out of the analyst's hands once alternative strategies are defined. Decisions regarding a particular DBMS, specific terminal types, and the automation of certain functions are often made more on political than technical bases.

The final step in preparing the new physical diagrams is to repartition the set of DFDs so that Figure 0 shows processes that are either
completely manual or completely automated, as in Figure 7.2. This
separation means that if there were a Layer 2 manual process called
Write Call Report and an automated process called Print Sales Summary, they would be subordinate to different Figure 0 processes because one is manual and the other automated. Separation of manual
from automated processes is more of a convenience than a necessity.
Since manual and automated systems are likely to be implemented by
completely separate groups in the company, this DFD partitioning is
helpful in allowing them to work independently.

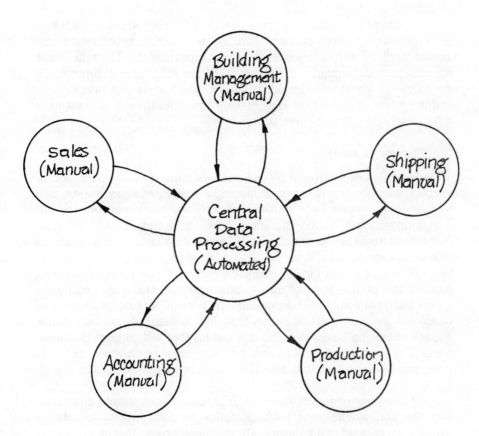

Figure 7.2. Example of a new physical DFD (Figure 0).

7.6 Completing the structured specification

Developing current DFDs, changing them to new logical DFDs, and finally rephysicalizing them is the technical work of structured analysis. After all this work comes the final step: completing and packaging the structured specification. This should be a straightforward process of assembling in one place all of the work done so far.

More specifically, to complete the structured specification, the developers assemble the new physical DFDs and project dictionary in a single place, and include documentation for management.

One such document is a short narrative overview of the system, stating its purpose, benefits, and costs. Depending on management needs, the specification may provide more complete documentation of scheduling and budget issues.

A second possible, albeit rare inclusion is descriptions of each major transaction. These are not part of the systems specification and should perhaps be packaged as a separate document. To write these transaction walkthroughs, the analyst follows the same techniques he would use in a real walkthrough. That is, he chooses one item of data and describes its processing step by step from the time it is input until it becomes one or more outputs.

7.7 The end of analysis

It is not unusual for a project team to come to the official end of analysis, even to the point of producing a structured specification, and to feel that analysis isn't finished. There are many reasons for not completing analysis within the allotted time and budget. Not the least frequent of these is the team's not being entirely sure what it means to "finish" analysis.

Wherever you are in the process of analysis, you have a document finished to a certain level of detail. Since the structured specification is a user document not a design document, it need be only as detailed as necessary to convince the user that the systems developers know enough about the business to build a system that will support that business. The amount of detail needed to do this varies widely, not only from project to project, but also from process to process within a project.

While preparing each level of DFD, the analyst should determine with the user whether the business policy for each process is detailed enough to proceed with design. If the user agrees that a process is described sufficiently, spend no more time on it, but go on to those that may not be so clear. I have seen much time wasted getting into the nuts and bolts of how a process is to be carried out when a simple two- or three-line structured English statement would have sufficed.

For example, it is hardly ever necessary to say more than Update Master File when the purpose is to make transactional changes to an existing file. I don't mean that sometimes you may not want to mention the treatment of duplicate transactions, or the addition of unmatched transactions. However, the basic techniques of a two-file merge are well known and need not be detailed in the structured specification.

Another reason for not being able to provide complete detail on a part of the analysis is that the user often is not sure of the detail. Because the steps in a structured analysis can be repeated, there is no reason a major piece of the system can't be left unanalyzed while the rest of the system is designed and implemented. Of course, the user will have to have the missing portion analyzed or deleted before the project is completed.

When the user is not sure of the detail of a process, the analyst's skill as an interviewer comes into play. I suggest that the analyst spend an afternoon talking with the users involved with the fuzzy area of the business. Frequently, the lack of clarity results from the user's not having thought about the subject at all, and just talking about it can clear the fog.

Making too many decisions regarding the new physical DFDs can also hinder the completion of analysis. According to the theory, the users must decide during analysis whether the system is to be online or offline, whether it is to use tapes or disks, whether processes are to be manual or automated, and so on. These certainly are decisions crucial to completion of the system.

However, while such physical constraints should be part of the new physical DFD, these decisions typically affect only the bottommost levels of a design structure chart. Frequently, physical constraints can be left out of analysis altogether and even ignored until well into design if necessary. With regard to DFDs, adding physical constraints often amounts to adding a few processes whose purpose is to transport data across physical boundaries. Seldom do they affect the underlying business philosophy being described by the structured specification.

Beyond providing a complete, unambiguous, and nonredundant specification of a user's business, the purpose of the structured specification is to enable a smooth transition to the design phase. To have finished analysis really means to be ready to start design, which the designers begin by drawing yet another level of even more physical DFDs. This is the first step in turning the structured specification into a design document; from these new DFDs the lowest levels of the design structure charts can be drawn. Additional details are typically incorporated into the structured English at this time, for example, the detail in an intricate update process.

Adding detail after completion of the structured specification should not be thought of as cheating. Rather, putting considerably more detail into design than into analysis is necessary, and there is no reason why users should not be involved in this part of the design process as much as they need to be.

7.8 Final exam

At this point, I have discussed the tools of structured analysis and the process of applying these tools to business problems. In order to help you solidify your understanding of the material, I include an exercise. This exam gives you a chance to develop a complete structured specification on a small but real system. You will need a partner to do this, although that person need not know anything about structured analysis.

In your group of two, one person acts as user and one as analyst. The user chooses one piece of paper that he knows how to process. The analyst then develops a structured specification for the processing of that piece of paper. I recommend you choose your MasterCard® or Visa® bill or a time sheet or some other familiar item.

When doing the exercise, try to be rigorous in developing the specification. Include data flow diagrams (layered if necessary), a project dictionary, and structured English for the processes. When you have finished, you may switch roles so that each of you has a chance to work both as user and analyst.

Finally, walk through your solution with the other person. To prepare for doing this, review the rules and conventions discussed earlier regarding DFD principles, layering, the project dictionary, and structured English.

7.9 Summary

The topic of structured analysis is now finished, except that, as in all real structured projects, there are always some things that could be done, or written, to make the final product more complete. In this case, the subject of database design needs further explanation, and this is best discussed now that you have a fairly complete outline of the tools and techniques of structured analysis. The next chapter offers the details of deriving a set of logical files to accompany the structured specification, which goes to a structured systems designer and to a physical database designer.

8

Database Design

The point at which database design begins may differ as much as any one structured project differs from another. Nevertheless, in order for database design to be most effective, project members should begin the task as soon as the first physical DFD is drawn and the project data dictionary is started.

The project dictionary represents the designer's entire current understanding of the project. It contains descriptions of every data structure, data element, process, and, most important, it contains an entry for *every* dataflow that appears on *any* DFD. It may even contain DFDs. Even if you don't know the complete definition of a dataflow, failure to enter it in the project dictionary is inviting chaos.

Bad dictionaries are usually inadequate for two reasons: First, not every dataflow is recorded in the project dictionary; and, second, the dictionary contains two or more defined names for the same data; these names are called *aliases*. The existence of aliases is not bad in itself; the difficulty arises when designers do not realize that multiple definitions refer to the same data. Unintentional aliases are difficult to detect since they may have slightly different definitions for the same data. Then, if the definition of an item changes, undetected aliases may not have their definitions changed to correspond. In such a case, the same item exists in the dictionary with two names and two quite different definitions, one of them obsolete.

In my experience, the single most common cause of difficulty in a structured project is lack of an up-to-date project dictionary. If at the time the designer formally begins database design the project dictionary is not complete and as clean as possible of aliases, proceeding with logical database design is somewhat futile, since extensive revisions will probably be necessary. Even if perfecting the dictionary extends the project by a month or more, begin database design only when a good project dictionary is available.

8.1 The logical database design

The theory of structured analysis tells us to eliminate implementation-dependent details of the current system whenever possible. This exhortation applies as much (or more) to files as it does elsewhere, simply because current technology encourages data files to accumulate redundant or obsolete data or files. The process of logical file derivation eliminates all obsolete data and minimizes redundancy. In structured analysis, a logical database is a set of files with the following characteristics:

- Each file has a unique key structure.* For example, if all records in Customer-Master-File are identified uniquely by Customer-Number, then Customer-Number is the key for this file and all information that is uniquely identified by Customer-Number appears in this file and in this file only.

- Each file has no repeating groups of data.† For example, if a history of sales to each customer contains the Customer-Number, Date-of-Transaction, and Amount-of-Sale for each sale, this information is stored in a separate logical file rather than appearing as a repeating group in the Customer-Master-File.

- Each file contains no information that can be derived from other information stored in the file.

---

*A key is that data element that is used to uniquely identify each record in a file. To access a certain record, a process must use the key. In some files, more than one data element is a key; the term *key structure* refers to all the keys of a file.

†These are the groups of data indicated by braces in a data dictionary format; a repeating group contains many different values that all describe the same type of data.

Files with these characteristics are said to be fully normalized. Analysts derive a set of fully normalized logical files from the physical files in the current system DFDs. They usually perform this step during the new logical phase of a structured analysis.

8.2 The derivation

Having to derive a set of logical files for the current system strikes terror into the heart of most analysts. Their feelings are not without justification, since in any reasonably sized system this can be a lengthy, cumbersome, and boring task. In the paragraphs that follow, I propose ways of making it manageable.

The process of deriving logical files requires the analyst to examine each file access. An access is the information requested from a file or, for updates, the information put into a file. It is represented by the line on a DFD that goes to or from a file. Each access may in fact contain only part of the information in a file.

This section looks at each step in the derivation process, giving a simplified way of doing it. I make two general observations that help to simplify file logicalization:

- Although a major system may involve several hundred different file accesses, the system often focuses on one area of the business, such as inventory, invoicing, or marketing. Because of this, most accesses typically use only a handful of different key structures, such as customer number, product number, and date. There may be a proliferation of small files with unique, two- or three-attribute key structures, but they will account for relatively few accesses.

- If I already have a set of logical files, in order to add an access to it, I can proceed by logicalizing that access and merging it into the existing file structures. I do not need to completely revise my previous work.

These observations allow me to proceed to a whole, logicalized file structure by normalizing one access at a time. That is, I can do something new without having to redo everything old.

Often a set of logical files can be developed intuitively. Nonetheless, studying the third-normal-form file derivation, as explained clearly by both DeMarco and Gane and Sarson, is worthwhile for the lead analyst on this phase of the project.* When it comes to justifying

---

*T. DeMarco, *Structured Analysis and System Specification* (New York: Yourdon Press, 1979), pp. 233-56; and C. Gane and T. Sarson, *Structured Systems Analysis: Tools & Techniques* (New York: Improved System Technologies, 1977), pp. 169-202.

shortcuts, there is no substitute for understanding the underlying theory.

Throughout the project the entire analysis group should regularly review the project dictionary to resolve aliases. This can be a time-consuming and chaotic process if aliases have been allowed to accumulate over a long period. If removed regularly, however, aliases need not be a problem at all. This kind of review is essential to a successful logical file derivation.

8.3 An example

So, how can we make logical file normalization a manageable task? That is, how can we do this job without endlessly writing and copying data? We proceed one access at a time, normalizing as we go and combining those results with previously normalized accesses. The result will be normalized files. The steps are discussed below:

1. Choose a single file access with which to work. It doesn't really matter which access is chosen, since all file accesses will be considered. Nevertheless, it sometimes makes sense to logicalize first those accesses that result in inputs to a process.

2. Do the following for each file access until all file accesses have been processed.

    a. Assign a number to the access and, using dictionary notation, list the data elements (not data structures) that are accessed.

    b. If any data elements in this access can be derived from other elements in this access, remove them. When step 2 is finished, we will have to remove derived elements again, but doing it once now reduces the magnitude of the task later on.

    c. Code the data elements for this access in terms of the access number. First, identify and underline each element that is a key of the access or a key of a repeating group of data elements. Then, using the access number and an additional sequence number, number each key and assign one number to the group of nonrepeating data elements related to a particular key. The following example shows a coded access:

Company Access 68 = {Company-Name + Sales + President + {Site-No. + Site-Name + {CPU}}}

68.1   68.2   68.3   68.4   68.5

d.   Using this encoded representation of the access, proceed to remove the repeating groups. That is, first create a new file containing the keys of the main access with its nonperiodic data elements only, and then create a new file for each periodic group, breaking down any file that still contains a repeating group. This gives us:

$$68' \quad - \quad \{\underline{68.1} + 68.2\}$$
$$68.3' \quad = \quad \{\underline{68.1} + \underline{68.3} + 68.4 + \{\underline{68.5}\}\}$$
$$68.3'' \quad = \quad \{\underline{68.1} + \underline{68.3} + 68.4\}$$
$$68.5' \quad = \quad \{\underline{68.1} + \underline{68.3} + \underline{68.5}\}$$

e.   Since new files have been created for the original file and file 68.3', these may now be discarded. Now replace the encoded keys (only) with their meanings and combine this new set of files with any previously normalized and combined files that have the same keys.

$$68' \quad = \quad \{\underline{\text{Company-Name}} + 68.2\}$$
$$68.3'' \quad = \quad \{\underline{\text{Company-Name}} + \underline{\text{Site-No}}. + 68.4\}$$
$$68.5' \quad = \quad \{\underline{\text{Company-Name}} + \underline{\text{Site-No}}. + \underline{\text{CPU}}\}$$

Let's say we have previously arrived at the following set of normalized files (NFs):

$$\text{NF1} = \{\underline{\text{Company-Name}} + 31.2\}$$
$$\text{NF2} = \{\underline{\text{Company-Name}} + \underline{\text{Site-No}}. + \underline{\text{CPU}} + 31.6\}$$

We now combine our new results based on common keys and come up with the following NFs:

NF1 and 68 give us a new

$$\text{NF1} = \{\underline{\text{Company-Name}} + 31.2 + 68.2\}$$

NF2 and 68.5' give us a new

$$\text{NF2} = \{\underline{\text{Company-Name}} + \underline{\text{Site-No}}. + \underline{\text{CPU}} + 31.6\}$$

NF2 is actually unchanged; no new data elements are required here since 68.5' contains nothing but keys.

Finally, since there is no existing file with Company-Name and Site-No. as the only keys, 68.3'' is simply added to the list of NFs.

$$\text{NF3} = \{\underline{\text{Company-Name}} + \underline{\text{Site-No}}. + 68.4\}$$

To further reduce later copying, the data element groups 31.2 and 68.2 could be combined to NF1.1 giving us

NF1 = {Company-Name + NF1.1}

f.   Now choose another single access and continue normalizing and combining.

3.   As a final step, or at any stage, replace the encoded data elements with their meanings and remove any elements that are duplicated or that can be derived from other elements.

8.4 Summary

By using this step-by-step incremental process, the designer can avoid much of the drudgery of deriving a set of logical files. Keep in mind, however, that the process of file normalization is sometimes unnecessary. This is true when the system has a relatively small number of files and the job can be done intuitively. If certain physical files are to be carried over into the new system, they also do not have to be logicalized.

Remember that the file normalization process is not intended to yield the most efficient file structure, only the minimal set of logical files needed for the system to have the accesses it needs. With a complete and nonredundant project dictionary, many designers attempt to finish logical database design by the time the new logical DFDs are complete.

As I said at the end of the last chapter, structured analysis is now complete, . . . or is it? When all of the diagrams have been drawn, the logical files derived, the process descriptions written, you are ready to move on to structured design. But the diagrams are never perfect, and the files could always be adjusted in some way. The beauty of structured analysis lies in the fact that at any stage you have a well-documented system that is finished to some extent, and that can be picked up and continued by another experienced structured analyst.

The entire process of diagramming and describing is intentionally designed to be an iterative and continuing one. Worry less about the finality of your specification, and focus on making sure that the work you have done is complete, unambiguous, and nonredundant. Above all else, keep the project dictionary up-to-date!

Conclusion

The foregoing chapters endeavor to transfer to analysts, users, and managers my hard-won understanding of the process of structured analysis as it applies in the real world. You should now have a better understanding of structured analysis, of both its tools and their application in the analysis process. However, as with any language or any discipline, you must practice regularly in order to become fluent.

To gain daily experience with structured analysis, try looking at everyday experiences as problems in structured analysis. By this, I mean the following: If you're sitting at your desk and someone hands you a piece of paper, imagine the situation represented by a DFD. Imagine the other person as a process that has put a piece of paper into one end of a dataflow, and imagine yourself as a process receiving the paper as an input. Looking at yourself as a process, be aware of what you do with that piece of paper; think about other inputs you may need, such as a pencil; and be aware of how a question and answer dialogue you may have with the person who gave you the paper resembles interaction with a database. When you finally dispose of the paper, try to look at its path as a dataflow to either a file or another process.

Structured analysis is a discipline applicable to nearly any problem. Its power lies in its facilities for organizing the technical details of a project's life cycle. Like most powerful mechanisms, structured analysis must be used with care and understanding. The results will be beneficial.

Whether you are a user, an analyst, or a manager, your attitude toward structured analysis is all-important in the successful completion of a project. Structured analysis requires of all project participants a thoroughness and care in handling detail that may seem strange and perhaps burdensome to those who are used to more traditional, relatively ad hoc approaches to systems development. If you understand the basic tools, the reasons for their development, and their practical

121

application, you will find the discipline of structured analysis to be liberating, and systems development to be a much more satisfactory activity.

My final advice is the same as my initial advice: Bring to bear on any project all of the wisdom you have gained in the past through developing, managing, and using systems to decide where the methods fit and where they don't.

Index

Access, file, 117-20
Aliases, 24, 42, 115-16, 118
Analysis phase, 7
   see also Structured analysis.

Balancing DFDs, 44ff., 89

Campbell, J., 6n.
Chapin chart, 69-70
CONDITIONAL construct, 59
Conservation rule, 27-29
Constantine, L., 10, 80
Context diagram, 94-95, 101-103
Cycle of change, 6-8

Data, 11, 13-25, 37
   notation to define, 16-20, 23
Database administrator, 20, 24
Database design, 72, 109, 115-20
   logical, 10, 77, 116-20
   physical, 77
Database management systems, 20, 24, 77, 110
Data dictionary: *see* Project dictionary.
Data element, 17-18, 22, 115, 118
Data flow diagram:
   balancing, 44ff., 89
   current logical, 50-53, 105-106
   file access in, 117

layering, 44-47, 55
management, 86-91
new functional, 108-10, 120
new physical, 79, 109-11
notation of, 26-27, 43, 56, 62
numbering convention, 46, 51, 54
project scheduling, 86-91
rules for drawing, 27-34, 43
Data structure, 17-18, 22, 115
Decision table, 63-66
Decision tree, 63-66
DeMarco, T., 10, 20, 44n., 72, 80, 108, 109, 117
Dickinson, B., 44n.
Documentation, 7, 9, 11, 21, 26

Feasibility document, 72-75, 102
Figure 0, 46-50, 83-84, 101-104, 111
Files, 22, 27, 33, 79
   accessing, 117-20
   balancing of, 49-50
   informational (logical), 2, 77, 109, 116-20
   physical, 15, 109, 117, 120

Gane, C., 10, 56, 62, 109, 117

Inclusive OR construct, 18
Independence rule, 31-32

Jackson, M., 10